I0473314

Guided

Beyond the paycheck
Practical steps to discovering
your Purpose.

Refilwe Marumo

Refilwe Marumo

Guided Beyond the Paycheck
Copyright © 2025 Refilwe Marumo
Published by: Mecs Publishing

www.mecspublishing-greenhornbooks.co.za
admin@mecspublishing-greenhornbooks.co.za

ISBN: 978-1-0492-4296-5

First published: 2025

Editing: Edna Cane Swannepoel
Formatting: Edna Cane Swannepoel
Cover design: Kingfisher Media Worx/Refilwe Marumo / Edna Cane Swannepoel

Print on demand.

Table of Contents

Acknowledgements

To Michelle Naude, my neighbour who welcomed me to our new neighbourhood in January 2025 and took an interest in me as if I were family. Within months of moving in, she lent me a book that told a beautiful story of hope when all seemed lost. It narrated how faith, despite the visible situation and against all odds, can give one a reason to live another day. She had no idea what I was going through, but that book helped a lot.

To Crina Nthabiseng Peter, a friend I met in 2022. Due to the numerous challenges, she had been experiencing that I had helped her navigate, we had grown very close. When I first confided in her about discovering my true calling—and the uncertainty I felt regarding the path forward—she offered the ultimate reassurance: that just as my purpose had been revealed, the means to achieve it would unfold in due time.

To Val Wagner, my across-the-road neighbour, A chance encounter with her, proved to be a pivotal turning point in my writing journey. What began as an afternoon invitation for coffee to help her review a series of word search puzzles soon revealed a series of remarkable coincidences. As Val explained that the puzzles were a companion to a book her employer had just written, she gifted me a copy and shared her own expertise in typesetting and cover design. At that moment, she had no way of knowing I was a first-time author grappling not with writer's block, but with the daunting uncertainty of how to bring my own manuscript to life. I returned home that afternoon and noted in my journal: 'Universe, what are you trying to tell me?'

A couple of weeks later, I got an invite from my "ride or die" friend, Mmabatho Mpshe. We met at university in 1998, both studying medical sciences. She majored in Genetics, and I majored in Microbiology. It was an instant connection, and we have been friends ever since, going through life's ups and downs together. The invite was to a book launch by her former boss, and Mmabatho felt it would be a great way to spend time together, as it had been a while since we did something just the two of us. Little did she know that I was having doubts and procrastinating over finishing mine. In fact, she had no idea I was busy writing a book; no one did.

These ladies had been sent to me at the time I needed affirmation the most. Embarking on this new journey was daunting, and there were many moments when one questioned whether to continue with this book. But their timely words and actions were powerful forms of validation during a period when the weight of this debut project felt overwhelming and that granted me the fortitude to keep going.

Dedication

To my family.

My son, Kitso, who introduced me to hiking on 31 December 2022, and I took to it like a duck to water; it became the biggest part of my healing journey. For a wise old soul, you are, thank you.

My daughter, Š, whose realistic views have the power to stop one dead in their tracks for a moment's thought. You're going to be a gentle guide to many.

My husband, Gladwin, for being my constant and reassuring anchor throughout the storm. As I navigated a difficult period of personal recalibration, your patience never wavered. Even during the months when I felt directionless and lost, you provided the steady support I needed to find my way again. You are my North Star

To Spin, our faithful 14-year-old companion, who insisted on our daily jogs. Beyond the exercise, those runs gifted me sunlight's vitamin D, the breath of fresh air, and a surge of dopamine—an unexpected chorus of happy hormones I hadn't realized my healing required.

To my wonderful mother, Lydia Nancy Maboko. Thank you for your motherly instincts in identifying my potential early on and doing everything in your power to ensure that I got the best possible education you could afford.

Foreword

When I first met Refilwe, I knew she would challenge the status quo. Her curiosity was relentless, her drive undeniable, but like so many high achievers, she was chasing milestones that looked impressive on paper yet left her soul starving. I've watched countless professionals climb ladders only to discover they're leaning against the wrong wall. Refilwe's story is proof that this realisation, though painful, can become the most powerful turning point of your life.

What you hold in your hands is not just a book, it's a roadmap drawn from lived experience. Refilwe doesn't preach theory; she shares scars and lessons earned in the trenches of business, burnout, and reinvention. She invites you to question the mould you've been handed, to listen to the quiet signals you've been ignoring, and to embrace the possibility that your purpose is not a distant dream, but a pattern already woven through your life.

As you read, you'll find practical tools, reflective exercises, and stories that will resonate deeply if you've ever asked, "Is this all there is?" My advice: don't rush through these pages. Sit with the questions. Let them disrupt your comfort zone.

Because the truth is, success without alignment is just survival, and you were made for more than that.

If you're ready to stop living someone else's definition of success and start crafting a life that feels authentic, this book is your starting point. Refilwe has done the hard work of turning pain into purpose; now she hands you the compass. Use it well

Preface

This book was born out of a collision between success and emptiness. For years, I chased every milestone society promised would bring happiness, the degree, the title, the pay cheque, only to find myself burned out and questioning everything. That quiet hum of dissatisfaction became impossible to ignore, and what followed was a journey through reinvention, resilience, and rediscovery.

GUIDED beyond the paycheck is not a manual for quitting your job overnight. It is a compass for anyone who feels misaligned, stuck in a mould that doesn't fit. Through personal stories, research, and practical exercises, I share how environmental shifts, serendipity, and even crises can become catalysts for uncovering your true calling. This is not about abandoning responsibility; it's about aligning your work with your soul's blueprint, where passion, talent, and purpose converge.

If you've ever wondered, *"is there more to life than this?"* this book is for you. I hope that these pages will help you pause, reflect, and take bold steps towards a life that feels authentic and fulfilling. Because purpose is not a luxury, it is the fuel that sustains us.

Introduction and Note to the Reader

Dear Reader,

You've hit every milestone society promised would bring happiness: the degree, the title, the big pay cheque. So why does it feel like you're starring in someone else's life? Why is there a constant, quiet hum of dissatisfaction you can't silence?

That hollow ache, the creeping burnout, the Sunday night dread, -- is your soul's contract trying to reach you. For years, like many others, you've suppressed it. In a world clouded by career demands, social status, economic and financial pressures, finding one's true purpose is often put on the back burner. Besides, would it even be sufficient to provide for your basic financial needs, let alone thrive?

This has led many of us to choose careers based on what is predicted as the next in-demand career, the most paying job, a big title, and the oh-so-glamorised corner office, rather than what feeds our souls. Unfortunately, this is often not aligned with our soul contracts and, in most cases, leaves us depleted, burned out, and depressed. No matter how much we put in, how high we climb that ladder, or how big our pay cheques grow, we just can't seem to get fulfilment. We're often so busy trying to get ahead that we can't fathom taking the time to pause and reflect on why we feel this way. Often, we think hitting another milestone, reaching another goal, or delivering another successful project will satisfy that craving and put it to bed. Well, if you're like me and nothing worked, if everything you tried still left you with a gaping hole and the wonder that there must be more to this, chances are you are not doing what you're called here to do. If so, this book is for you.

Here, we're going to journey together to explore the many common ways you can identify, ultimately embrace, and embody your true purpose. Perhaps you have found yourself asking the same fundamental questions: Does a true calling actually exist? Where does the search begin? And how will I recognize it once it is found?

Rest assured, this sense of purpose is very real.

Upon its discovery, you will likely find yourself struck by its inherent familiarity. It feels natural—an intuitive alignment so seamless you may wonder how it eluded you for so long. We live in a world where personal identity is often subsumed by parental expectations or societal definitions of success; do not fault yourself for momentarily burying your inner drive. Reclaiming your purpose is the most transformational milestone you will ever experience.

A clear sense of purpose is more than a goal; it is existential fuel—a definitive reason to navigate the complexities of life. While some are fortunate enough to identify their path early, others require a map. If you are among the former, I invite you to enjoy this book as a reflective companion. If you are still searching, may these pages serve as the compass that leads you home

The questions and the pain are signals: That feeling of depletion and lack of fulfilment, despite external success, is the strongest evidence that you are off purpose.

1. The anti-purpose trap: Choosing a career based on social status, money, or perceived demand--the "mould", is the fastest path to burnout.

2. Discovery vs creation: Purpose is not a job you invent; it is a unique calling you must discover and align with.

Refilwe Marumo

Part 1

The Inner Compass

Chapter 1:

What is Purpose?

Imagine waking up every day with a profound, quiet certainty: *This is what I am meant to do.* Not for the salary, not for the status, but for the sheer fuel it gives your existence. This feeling—this existential fire—is Purpose. The Japanese call it *Ikigai,* the secret to a long and happy life, A REASON FOR BEING. But for most of us, this feeling is crushed by the great societal mold we are forced into...

- We're Born
- Grow up--formative years where most beliefs are instilled (nurture)
- Go to school
- Get a degree
- Find a job,
- Work till retirement

Of course there's a lot of other things that fall in-between, like— getting married, getting a house, having children etc, We're mostly a product of nurture and most of our identity and beliefs –good or bad are instilled in us at an early age and tend to shape the rest of our lives unless something drastic happens or conscious effort is exercised to change the course of things.

Erik Erikson's Stages of Psychosocial Development beautifully outlines the eight developmental stages in a person's life. It illustrates that at each stage; a person experiences a psychosocial crisis that must be navigated to acquire basic virtues and develop a healthy personality. The theory highlights the influence of social interactions and experiences across a person's entire lifespan, suggesting that personality development is an ongoing process. How your needs or key events were met at each developmental stage determines whether you would have acquired good or bad virtues. In this case, I would apply this to how your environment and exposure can inform the career path you choose, and most of the time, this may have nothing to do with your inner calling. See Table 1.1 hereunder for further details.

Erikson's Eight Stages of Psychosocial Development

Stage	Approximate Age	Psychosocial Crisis	Key Events	Outcome/ Virtue
1	Infancy (Birth to 18 months)	**Trust vs. Mistrust**	Feeding, consistent care	**Hope**: A sense of security and trust that basic needs will be met.
2	Early Childhood (18 months to 3 years)	**Autonomy vs. Shame and Doubt**	Toilet training, self-care	**Will**: A sense of independence and self-control.
3	Preschool (3 to 5 years)	**Initiative vs. Guilt**	Exploration, play, and asking questions	**Purpose**: The ability to initiate activities and feel capable.
4	School Age (6 to 11 years)	**Industry vs. Inferiority**	School, social activities	**Competence**: A sense of pride and accomplishment

				in abilities and work.
5	Adolescence (12 to 18 years)	**Identity vs. Role Confusion**	Social relationships, peer influence	**Fidelity:** A strong sense of self and personal values.
6	Young Adulthood (19 to 40 years)	**Intimacy vs. Isolation**	Romantic relationships, commitment	**Love:** The ability to form close, committed relationships with others.
7	Middle Adulthood (40 to 65 years)	**Generativity vs. Stagnation**	Work, parenthood, mentoring	**Care:** The desire to contribute to society and guide the next generation.
8	Late Adulthood (65 years to death)	**Integrity vs. Despair**	Reflection on life	**Wisdom:** A sense of satisfaction and acceptance of

				one's life as a whole.

Table 1.1 Source: Simply Psychology

So how does this then affect or shape your purpose? Your environment might shape your beliefs, how you conduct yourself, and how you identify opportunities. Let's take for instance someone growing up in a family with a business such as a bakery, becoming a baker seems logical. Then you hear stories that it has been in the family for generations, like being a baker is hereditary, or that of a young man becoming a policeman just because his father was one and that inspired him. In the community I grew up in, every house around us had a policeman and a nurse; in fact, my parents were the only ones with different professions at the time, and this persisted for years and led to a second generation of policemen. Many remained in their profession until retirement, and many other similar stories will be demonstrated further in the following chapters. Still, this environmental influence can never silence your true calling.

An irresistible personal pull towards a specific pursuit that gives life meaning. That one thing you find yourself drawn to over and over again, even if it comes camouflaged in different forms. The one thing you'd happily do even if you weren't getting paid…and I'm not talking doom scrolling or TV binge watching here, I'm talking about that which, if you found, would ignite the quest to fulfil your destiny. That which motivates you to be and do your best, sometimes even against all odds.

It is your unique calling—your primary assignment for the impact you're meant to make. It gives direction to your innate talents and the skills you may have acquired. Most importantly, it is meant for others.

The difference between these three, talent, skills, and purpose, is that talents are one's natural abilities and aptitude. Talents form part of the tools required to fulfil your purpose. Whilst skills are acquired through deliberate effort, learning, and practice. Talents can also lie dormant if not applied and fine-tuned through practice. Your purpose may even guide you towards the skills you'll need to fulfil your primary assignment, if you are tuned in. The mistake most of us make is looking for work based on the skills we have acquired through our chosen career paths, rather than on our talents and purpose.

The Difference Between Career and Life Purpose

Life purpose goes far beyond what you do for a living. It speaks to the deeper meaning behind your existence, a guiding force that shapes your choices and gives fulfilment on a personal level. While careers often focus on specific skills and income, life purpose involves aspects of identity, values, relationships, and legacy. It answers questions about why you wake up each day and what impact you hope to have on the world around you. For many, understanding their life purpose brings a sense of clarity and direction that isn't tied solely to job titles or promotions.

This purpose might involve contributing to a community, nurturing creativity, fostering connection, or advocating for causes that feel meaningful. It often includes a combination of passions and beliefs that motivate individuals, even when the path isn't always clear or financially rewarding. Recognizing life purpose can also provide resilience during difficult times, offering a bigger picture that supports perseverance beyond the pressures of work and achievement. In this way, life purpose plays a central role in overall well-being and happiness, touching every corner of daily experience rather than remaining confined to professional goals.

Career and life purpose are related but not interchangeable. A career typically refers to the progression of jobs, roles, or activities through which people earn a living or gain professional recognition. It is often shaped by external factors such as market demand, education, and skill development. While some find deep satisfaction in their work, others' career decisions are driven mainly by financial needs or social expectations. A career might change multiple times in one's life as interests shift or opportunities arise, without necessarily touching on what someone feels they were meant to do on a deeper level.

In contrast, life purpose is broader and more enduring. Job descriptions or income levels do not limit it as it relates closely to personal identity and meaning. For example, a teacher might have a career focused on education, yet their life purpose could include inspiring others, supporting growth, or advancing equality. A business leader's purpose may involve fostering innovation or creating inclusive environments rather than just climbing the corporate ladder. Understanding this difference helps people avoid confusing their job role with their entire sense of self. It encourages reflection on what truly matters beyond daily work routines and professional achievements.

It's also common for individuals to pursue careers that serve as tools to fulfil their life purpose rather than being their purpose itself. A social worker, an artist, or a scientist may all follow very different career paths but share a similar motivation to solve problems, express ideas, or improve lives. Recognizing this distinction can lead to more intentional decisions, ensuring career choices support rather than detract from broader life goals. Sometimes, this awareness helps people shift direction or integrate multiple aspects of their identity, rather than feeling trapped in a single role.

One way to think about it is that a career is often about "what" you do, while life purpose is about "why" you do it. Careers can provide structure, resources, and experiences, but a life purpose gives them meaning and coherence over time. People who align their careers with their life purpose tend to experience greater satisfaction, but it remains possible and common for these areas to be distinct. Understanding this allows for flexibility and acknowledges that life's purpose can remain constant even if career paths evolve or change completely.

Reflecting on your life purpose alongside your career can reveal gaps or opportunities for growth. It might inspire you to seek roles that better reflect your values or to cultivate interests outside of work that contribute to your sense of fulfilment. Even small actions or side projects aligned with your life purpose can improve your emotional well-being and motivation. Viewing career and life purpose as parts of a larger whole encourages balance, recognizing that neither alone can define a full, meaningful life experience.

Why Discovering Your Purpose Matters for Long-Term Fulfilment

Understanding your purpose provides a strong foundation for feeling truly fulfilled in life. When you know what drives you—what gives your life meaning—you build a clear sense of direction. This sense of purpose acts as a guiding light, helping you stay focused and motivated even when faced with challenges. Without it, daily routines can feel hollow, and accomplishments may seem superficial or short-lived.

Discovering your purpose isn't just about having a career goal or a big dream; it's about connecting with what makes you feel alive and purposeful. It influences your decisions, your relationships, and your overall mindset. When your actions align with your core values and passions, life feels more authentic and satisfying. This alignment naturally leads to a sense of peace and contentment that isn't easily shaken by setbacks.

Having a clear purpose also acts as a buffer against stress and obstacles. When you're aware of why you do what you do, setbacks are less discouraging because they're seen as part of a larger journey. With purpose, failures become stepping stones rather than dead ends. You're more resilient because your inner motivation sustains you through difficult times, rather than relying solely on external validation or circumstances.

Long-term fulfilment is closely tied to this sense of purpose because it provides stability over time. Material gains or fleeting pleasures might provide momentary happiness, but they don't create lasting satisfaction. Purpose, on the other hand, offers a deeper sense of meaning that persists regardless of changing external conditions. It helps you to view life as a continuous pursuit of growth, contribution, and genuine happiness rather than a series of disconnected achievements.

Knowing your purpose also helps clarify what truly matters in your life. It encourages you to prioritize activities, relationships, and goals that resonate with your core identity. This clarity often leads to making more meaningful choices, reducing unnecessary stress or distraction caused by pursuits that don't truly excite or fulfil you. Over time, this alignment results in more genuinely and contentedly living—one that sustains you through both good times and bad.

Once you discover your purpose, it can serve as a compass during difficult moments. When life becomes complicated or unpredictable, having a clear sense of why you do what you do helps you stay grounded. It reminds you that setbacks are temporary and that your true fulfilment comes from living in line with your inner values. Cultivating this awareness can lead to a sense of peace and inner strength that provides stability well beyond external circumstances.

Additionally, discovering your purpose often leads to increased engagement in your daily life. It makes activities more meaningful and work more satisfying because you see how what you do contributes to something larger than yourself. When your work or hobbies align with your purpose, they stop feeling like chores and become fulfilling parts of your journey. This, in turn, nurtures a sustained sense of happiness that doesn't fade easily.

Focusing on your purpose also encourages long-term thinking. Instead of chasing quick wins or temporary pleasures, you begin to consider what will bring lasting satisfaction. This perspective not only improves your overall well-being but also helps you set realistic goals that align with your deeper values. The result is a life built around consistency, meaning, and growth, which can sustain you for decades.

For anyone seeking more meaningful and lasting happiness, taking time to reflect on what truly matters can be transformative. Making small, intentional choices guided by your purpose daily can gradually deepen your sense of fulfilment. Remember, discovering your purpose is an ongoing process, not a one-time event. Regularly revisiting and refining your understanding of what matters keeps your journey authentic and aligned with your evolving self.

The Great "Un-Molding"

In recent years, we're seeing a bit of change simmering in the workplace. A new trend is emerging in which millennials seem to not quite fit into the workplace mold and are rejecting the status quo. Research shows that they demand more flexibility, a better work-life balance, (MuchSkills). They prioritize mental health over pay increases and titles. They seek work that aligns with their values, leading companies to focus more on social responsibility and ethical practices, according to QES-Academy and Deloitte Insights. They are redefining the rules of engagement. This seems to have sparked, or even rekindled, the question that had lain dormant for years in most people, some kind of awakening. Let's look at what's at the heart of this awakening, starting with the origins of the concept of working for money.

Evidence of wage labour can be traced back as far as 5000 years, but the modern-day concept of working for money evolved from barter and gifting to what became known as the Industrial Revolution, as labour became commodified and sold. It emerged in Europe around the 16th century from the landless peasantry resulting from the enclosure of common land, making it hard for people to sustain themselves, and they were left with no option but to sell their labour.

"What impact did this work-for-money concept have on purpose?"

Evidently, it created a conflict between Intrinsic factors, driven by the internal desire to engage in an activity purely because it is inherently enjoyable and aligned with one's personal values, which often leads to long-term engagement, personal growth, and fulfilment. And the Extrinsic factors, those in which one engages in an activity purely for external rewards, such as money or accolades, or to avoid punishment, which are not sustainable but can be effective in the short term.

This transition to working for money has both positive and negative impacts. Still, as soon as people discover that money alone as a motivator is not enough, and this normally happens as soon as basic needs are met, other elements must come into play for a wholesome existence. And it would seem the millennials have had this realization and are out to correct this.

The work of **Viktor Frankl's Logotherapy** emphasizes that we don't create meaning, we discover it, and that excessive striving can prevent fulfilment. We look at the Core Principles of his teaching:

- Humans are primarily motivated by a search for purpose, not just pleasure or power.

- We don't create the meaning of our life—we discover it.

- We each have a unique reason for being, which can be adjusted or transformed many times over the years.

- The side of the equation we end up on depends on our decisions, not on the condition in which we find ourselves.

Purpose is defined as an **irresistible personal pull** that gives life meaning (Ikigai). It is our existential fuel, often suppressed by the rigid **"societal mold"**—the predictable path of school, degree, job, and retirement. But we have the power to change this, and the millennials have ignited this.

1. **Purpose is Discovery, Not Invention:** You don't make up your purpose; you uncover what is already unique to you (per Logotherapy).

2. **The Mold is Not Mandatory:** The rigid career path imposed by society is actively rejected by younger generations, driven by the search for own sense of alignment.

3. **The Opposite of Purpose:** The opposite of finding purpose isn't misery, but a focus on the wrong things—hyper-intention on a desire (like money or status) can actually block fulfilment.

Chapter 2

The Path that leads to it

What happens when the path laid out for you—the one you worked tirelessly for—suddenly feels like a dead end? For me, that road ran straight through the dusty, underdeveloped streets of Soshanguve and into a Microbiology lab. The first sign that I was off course wasn't a revelation; it was an escalating series of culture shocks that began when I was fifteen. In this chapter, we explore how the forces that *break* you can also be the ones that ultimately *shape* the path to your purpose. You see, I, like many others, didn't know that I had a unique purpose. In fact, I don't think I ever thought about it until my first job after graduating with a Microbiology Degree in 2002. I just remember feeling some resistance to what I was doing as a profession at the time. But let me share the journey that led to that.

I grew up in a township called Soshanguve. A settlement in the North of Pretoria, South Africa, created for the **So**tho's,

Shangaan's, **Nguni**'s, and **Venda**'s. Townships were established far on the outskirts of the cities for blacks by the apartheid government. These were mostly underdeveloped and had the bare minimum of services. And so, by default, I went to township schools, which offered substandard education. Over and above that, anyone who grew up in the township knows that there's not much else outside the classroom in terms of extramural activities. So, my school years were mostly defined by academic performance. I was doing fairly well, often coming out first or second in class. The issue is that at that age, one never got to experience any activities that might have given a window into other talents, if any.

It did not take long for my parents to realize that I had potential, and that this environment might stifle it. As much as my mom never finished school, she valued education, and she went out of her way to give me the best she never had. So, for my grade 10 in 1995, she enrolled me at a school, Willowridge High in the affluent white people's suburbs, some 60km away from home. This was what was called a Model C school post-apartheid, and blacks could now be accepted at what were previously white-only schools.

"Apartheid was a system of institutionalized racial segregation and discrimination in South Africa from 1948 to 1994, enforced by the all-white government of the National Party. It classified people into racial groups and dictated that non-white South Africans live in separate areas, use separate facilities, and have their rights severely limited. The term "apartheid" translates from Afrikaans to "apartness," and the system formalized discrimination into a rigid legal code that stripped the majority population of political and social power.

- **Control and oppression:** *Non-whites were denied the right to vote and had to carry passes to move between areas. The government used brutal methods to suppress dissent and resistance, which groups like the African National Congress led.*

- **International condemnation and eventual end:** *Growing internal and international pressure, including economic sanctions, led to the gradual dismantling of apartheid laws in the late 1980s and early 1990s. Nelson Mandela was released from prison, negotiations began, and the first multiracial democratic*

> *elections were held in 1994, with Mandela becoming*
> *president.*
>
> *Source: South African History online*

The power of exposure

Now, apart from the early mornings where one had to wake up in the wee hours, to take a bus that seemed to go on forever just to get to the school on time, and the same in the afternoon just to get home around 5 pm, one also experienced an awakening. A whole new world had just opened up! A big shift, so different in so many ways, that it had a huge impact on how the rest of my life would be shaped. Let me share a few.

Just stepping off the bus in the suburbs, my 15-minute walk to the school would be a showcase of luxury, I had never witnessed. Houses so big and of different architectural styles, remember township houses were all the same design and small. There'd be a few here and there that would be extended, and that's how you knew the family was doing better than the rest. The manicured lawns, beautifully

23

curated gardens, each house with a car or multiple vehicles, and all streets tarmacked. This looked absolutely beautiful, and I was just in awe.

At the school, of course, the premises were just as beautiful: a big, imposing Admin block and paved grounds. Big lawn gardens and, you've guessed it, sporting facilities. As if that was not enough, there was a half-Olympic-sized swimming pool, and I was glass-eyed because I had never seen anything like it, and of course, I didn't know how to swim.

For the first time, I had a blazer, a tie, and sporting gear, which included a swimming costume. I now had extracurricular activities! You see, this was compulsory here, and I loved the variety and the good mix of sporting and cultural activities. The philosophy was clearly to nurture the whole person, academically, physically, and culturally; it was all important here.

This, of course, did something magical to my outlook. I remember having to carry my big school bag and a sports duffel bag, all dressed in my tie and blazer. There's something psychological that happens to one the minute you don a tie and a blazer. The way you walk, how you

24

conduct yourself, your thought process, and your perception of self all change, and that's when I knew that I would never be the same again.

Well, that excitement was soon tempered by the first few weeks of school. Being in a classroom with mixed races and being taught primarily in English (no African mother-tongue explanations here), an attempt would be made to clarify some concepts, but this would often be in Afrikaans, another white folks' language, which we only took as a peripheral subject in the townships. In fact, Afrikaans was what led to the Soweto student uprising in the mid 70's, and so it had been toned down a lot in schools by the time I was of school age. Having to focus hard on grasping the teacher's accents and the pace of teaching, my grades took a knock, and of course, with that, my confidence. I had overnight gone from being an A student at a township school to a C, occasionally skating on a thin D. There were a lot of tears and many sleepless nights. Devastating was an understatement. Did I mention that the school wasn't free? And so, the thought that my parents took me out of a no-fee school (yes, substandard, I know) to now pay what seemed like thousands per month for this! a C-!

Not only was it going pear-shaped academically, but also in sport. Physical Education went from an exciting thought to some kind of torture in reality. I was, of course, unfit, didn't know how to swim, and found the water freezing for my liking. I'd always think to myself, "it's 9:00 in the morning! What do you mean, jump into the pool?!" And so, it was not long before I started fishing for excuses to go to the sick room, another new thing I had discovered. That one can actually fake sickness, go to the sick room, and sleep the day away! Only in the burbs! You see, my parents worked far from the school, they didn't have a car and couldn't be called to pick me up—ah bliss. But this faking didn't last long as I started getting sick for real. I started suffering from terrible bouts of Migraines so bad that I landed in the hospital several times.

Things were just as wobbly outside the classroom. You see, I was dealing with a double-edged sword here. That of being new (anyone who's switched schools mid-high school knows what I mean) and being of colour. Don't get me wrong, the school had a few other learners of colour, but making friends didn't happen on day one, and so, for a while, break time was lonely. But then one day, I made a friend, and slowly but surely, the adjustment happened, and my experience started changing.

Within weeks, I learnt how to swim; my PT teacher was that good. I mean, this is the same school that had the likes of Olympic swimmer and multi-gold medallist, Roland Schoeman, in my grade. Now you understand. I got physically fit; I got involved in the Rotary Club. I signed up for cultural activities such as drama and participated in school beauty pageants. Then something interesting happened! I became popular! By Grade 11, I had been selected as a Prefect. Quite a milestone considering I had been there for just under 12 months.

Talent meets skills.

The prefects had to attend a leadership camp to bond and learn leadership skills before taking up the role. This was also my first. I had never been to camp, but I loved it. I loved being in nature, the obstacle courses, and the camaraderie. I remember the next morning being served muesli with yogurt as part of a breakfast spread, and my delight at discovering such a cereal. I was 16! "Where had that been all my life?!" To this day, muesli remains one of

27

my favourites and a staple in my house. All in all, camp was great, full of new experiences and discoveries. Here, what was just leadership potential had been sharpened and equipped with practical skills, and one felt ready to lead fellow learners.

Back at school, things were good too; my confidence was at an all-time high, and my grades had drastically improved. Being a Prefect also meant you got to wear stockings and kitten heels. You stood out, which sort of gave you an authority mentality and the ability to issue little instructions to keep other learners in check. Again, the impact this "power suit energy" had on me was palpable. I would respect the dress code as a powerful tool well into my business years. The term power-dressing is a phenomenon that triggers a psychological effect known as enclothed cognition, where the symbolic meaning of clothes influences the wearer's mental state. Ever noticed how you feel when dressed in your work clothes versus when dressed in your gym clothes? Or how you immediately can guess a singer's music genre if they show up in baggy jeans, chains and teeth grills? And so I suppose that is why we have different clothes for different activities because clothing has the power to influence your behaviour. Studies show that wearing formal or authoritative attire can enhance critical thinking, sharpen focus and increase attention to detail. Just like how stepping into a "powersuit" can act as a psychological armour, improving posture and making the wearer feel more assertive, decisive and in control.

By Grade 12, I was deputy head girl, still juggling a few other things, and had been accepted at university. Life was good. But it is fascinating how a change in environment can act as a hard reset for the human mind and often turning a person's life in a new direction. History has many such stories of the change that was brough about by exposure to either a new religion or relocation. Take for instance the story of Marie Curie. Marie Curie (born Maria Skłodowska) provides a powerful look at how a change in environment can unlock scientific genius that was being suppressed. Living in Russian-occupied Poland, Maria was barred from higher education because she was a woman. To study, she had to attend the "Flying University," an underground, secret educational enterprise. In 1891, she moved to Paris to attend the Sorbonne. In Paris, she was desperately poor—legend says she sometimes fainted from hunger—

29

but she had something she never had in Warsaw: unfettered access to laboratories and the best scientific minds of the age. The move shifted her from an underground student to a pioneer of radioactivity. She met Pierre Curie, and together they discovered Polonium (named after her homeland) and Radium. Her relocation didn't just change her life; it changed the periodic table and the future of medicine.

While controversial, Elon Musk's move at age 17 is a textbook case of how a change in environment can unlock a specific type of ambition. Born in Pretoria, Musk left for Canada (and later the U.S.) to avoid mandatory military service in the Apartheid-era South African Defence Force.

Musk has often noted that the "can-do" culture of Silicon Valley was the only environment where his radical (and expensive) ideas for SpaceX and Tesla could have survived.

The move shifted him from a bright, somewhat alienated student in a restrictive society to an entrepreneur in the most aggressive venture capital environment in the world. He is a prime example of "Human Capital" finding the right "Soil" to grow in.

The change is what psychologists termed the Expat effect; When you move or change religions, the "scripts" you've been following no longer work. This forces your brain into a state of high neuroplasticity, making you more creative and open to radical shifts in identity.

When you move from a disadvantaged background to an affluent, high-resourced environment/ school like I did, the impact is rarely a simple upward trajectory. Instead, it creates a complex psychological and social phenomenon that despite the initial trauma of the move, one often emerges with a unique "superpower." Because they have navigated two vastly different social classes, they become highly adept at perspective-taking. Like a traveller who has lived in two countries, they can "read" different social environments better than those who have only ever lived in the "bubble" of affluence.

Although my move was not of these great proportions, it had a positive impact nonetheless and I was most grateful for the experience, the transition, and all that I had learnt even about myself. I discovered that I'm a resilient, adaptable, and strong-willed young woman able to take on anything, all thanks to the value of a holistic environment.

Purpose is often revealed not through direct pursuit but through **environmental shifts and extreme challenges** that can result in **dramatic personal awakening**. The experience demonstrated the importance of a **holistic environment** (academic, physical, cultural) in nurturing full potential.

1. **Your Environment is Key:** The path to purpose requires an environment that nurtures the **whole person,** not just academic or professional skills.

2. **Failure as Forge:** Resilience is not an innate trait but is **forged by enduring difficult transitions** (the C-grades, the loneliness). These hard times reveal the inner strength necessary for purpose.

3. **Explore Beyond the Box:** Limiting yourself to only one type of activity (like academics) can stifle the discovery of other **talents, passions, and life skills** that form the foundation of your future calling.

Chapter 3

The green flags

Towards the end of my Microbiology degree, there were already signs that this might not actually be what I wanted for a career. Spending countless hours between white walls, in a white coat, peering down a microscope at microbes that did not converse was not my idea of fun. I literally felt my joy being sucked right out of me. To think that I thought I'd be the one to discover HIV cure— "What was I thinking?!" I mean, look at me, I am vibrant, full of energy, like talking to anyone and everyone about anything and everything type of girl. I can strike up a conversation with a total stranger and talk to them about a subject they raised, as if I were an expert in it. "This does not feel right."

That was the moment I knew I had to change direction. Yes, there had been career guidance at the school level and so forth, but to be honest, I got into Microbiology because my mom used to work for the Medical Research Council of South Africa, and growing up, she'd often take me to work during school holidays. I fell in love with the idea of being a scientist when I saw how sophisticated those in their lab coats looked —like they were about to save the world or something. Well, I guess they do save lives. But now being here, No! Not for me, thanks.

I was still not clear which path would be best next. I mean, it took student loans and several years of studying to get here, and now to have to change it was a mammoth ask, but one thing was certain: I was not staying here. It felt like a total misfit, and I had to save myself and get out fast.

This is the moment when your inner GPS starts flashing. It wasn't a dead-end, but clear signals. In this chapter, we explore those subtle, irresistible forces I call the 'green flags'—the moments that affirmed where I *should* be going.

Failure - a stepping stone

It was during these years that I got married, and so when I fell pregnant with my first child, Kitso in 2003, I took the time out to reflect on and plan my next move. Two years later, I got back into the working world armed with a business plan, guts and no experience and started a corporate cleaning business. Luckily, I got clients within 6 months, initially from businesspeople I knew through association and networking. I hired cleaning staff and did placements, and within a year, more clients had signed up. I had to learn how to run a business, do HR, and accounting all on the fly. I literally built wings when the plane had already taken off.

The business kept me busy and allowed me to interact with different people daily—something I had been craving. I'd pay visits to clients' offices to do quality checks; I'd engage with them to assess whether they were happy and whether there was anything else we could do. This was going well in terms of scratching the itch.

A couple of years later, I was approached by my husband's colleague from the Telecommunications industry (broadcasting, to be exact), asking us to partner to apply for a Radio Frequency License that ICASA (Independent Communications Authority of South Africa) was issuing. Of course, my response was that I knew nothing about Radio, but he wasn't fazed. The fact that I was already running a stable, albeit small business was good enough for him. He proposed that I would be in charge of the business side, and he'd look after the broadcasting side. After much thought and reading the proposal, I got interested. Together with a bigger team, we put together an application, but unfortunately, we were not successful. However, for me, the whole application process, the exposure to the industry, the mountain of research we had to do for market study, the events, the socializing, and a glimpse of what was possible, grabbed me. The energy I felt during that process, the joy! All that made me think, "this must be it! This must be where I'm supposed to be".

Life continued for a while, and then, several years later, ICASA released a few more frequencies. Because the bug had bitten, I got involved with another team and again dedicated hours to putting the application together and even went to the extent of taking funds from the cleaning business to finance the application process. I was invested. Unfortunately, we did not win the license again in this round. It was devastating and made me question whether this was really where I was meant to be. Doubt crept in, and I decided to let it go and start afresh. With no cash flow, I asked the client companies to absorb some of the cleaners, and luckily, most were happy to. I deregistered the business with SARS and decided to go get a job. Perhaps I was just not cut out for business.

Inner GPS

One Easter, I went looking for a church because my children, aged 8 and 4 at the time, especially the 8-year-old, had been asking what Easter was about. I mean, we observed Easter and special holy days like most families do, but my kids had no background to this, had never been baptized, let alone set foot in church. Why or how? you might ask. Well, I walked out of church at the age of 11. As soon as I found my voice, I challenged a whole lot of things, traditions, cultural practices, and religion. Thinking about it now, I gave my poor mom such grief. I was never the "yes, ma'am" or be seen and not heard type of child. She could never just say "that's how it has always been", although she tried many times to throw the "as long as you're under my roof" line. It soon became clear that, unlike my older siblings, I was not going to get confirmed, and I dropped out of church. I still wonder how I pulled that off, but I'm grateful they never locked me out of the house every time they went to church.

Anyway, in a funny twist of fate, some 20 years after I walked out of church, I found myself back on this one good Friday, after driving into the parking lot of the first church we came across. My mission-- to grin and bear the service so I can give my kids context of the Easter celebration. To my surprise, the service was good. The Priest was warm and welcoming. The sermon and interpretation thereof did not carry the message that we're all sinners, no matter what we do. You know, the types that made me leave church in the first place, but rather reassuring and inspirational. I put this down to the fact that it was Easter; the priest knew there'd be lots of visitors during this period on the church calendar, and he was just being nice. Church is not usually like this. I thought to myself.

Needless to say, we went back 2 days later on Easter Sunday and had such a lovely time that we became regular visitors. By the start of the 3rd month, the priest announced that they were looking for additional Sunday school teachers, and like an old TV ad, "beware the kick" was the tag line-- where a

little man kicks one from under a chair which then propelled
the one seated to shoot straight up, I found my hand raised
high, and I swear I had lost control of my reflexes,
something else was moving me. With no time wasted, I was
signed up, trained, certified, and within a couple of weeks, I
was a Sunday school teacher. Several years later, I even had
the opportunity to head up the Sunday school ministry, and
I took the opportunity to introduce a few new things. I went
on to establish the Sunday School Marimba band, that
participated in two International Marimba festivals. At the
time, we were the only church group to have participated in
this festival. Most of the entrants were from school groups.
Our group also had the youngest member at the festival
because our Sunday school took in children from age 4. The
joy and pride this brought to the children and their parents
were reward enough for all the Saturday mornings
sacrificed. Marimba became a staple of our church events.

A few years later, I got approval from the priest at the time,
Father X as he was affectionately known, to establish what
I called the Church University, with a teaching format that
was different from Sunday School, engaging and filled with
youth relevant activities to address the purge of the kids who

39

were at the "beyond Sunday school age", but still too young for big church (15-19 years). As a church, we were blessed to have a Priest like him, forward-thinking, a visionary, with the children's interests at heart. The man was in the right space, he led the flock with delicate care and balance, knowing how to forge relations, when to listen to the congregants and when to take the lead. Under his watch the church was progressive and vibrant. He restored my faith in the church. He was the one who was preaching that fateful good Friday, the reason I stayed and got involved and I believe I was not the only one-- his influence touched many others. It was common knowledge that he had left the life of a banker to be a priest. Undoubtedly, a purpose fuelled move. He took the time to read my proposal, understood and endorsed my vision, and gave the go-ahead even though this grade did not exist within the Diocese ministry structures. This initiative, affectionately known as UNI, became so successful that we were able to attract this age group back to church. A balanced mix of lessons, skills development programme, and fun activities that one had planned and was delivering to this age group resonated, and the numbers kept growing.

Again, my Saturday mornings got filled with me imparting skills like playing the marimba (an African xylophone). Heat-pressing/ merchandize branding, marketing, and sales for fundraising. This helped the UNI generate funds for their annual year-end camp, and of course, that gave them drive and made them goal oriented. They'd work hard printing church logos on to merchandise like hoodies, mugs, and travel bottles once I informed them that all proceeds would be theirs. They would then market and sell these to congregants after church, and every month-end, we would do a financial review to see how much their sales had generated. At the end of the year, they got to go on a fully paid camp, including transport, food, and activities. The only thing they had to ask their parents for, was permission to go. The realization of what they were capable of achieving was priceless. They loved it.

They also got to learn other skills such as woodwork, gardening, presentations, etc., most of which I self-taught or called in an expert once or twice to learn just enough so I could onward teach. I became some kind of a Jack of all trades, and as you know, the rest of the saying...

41

Teaching these youngsters filled me with such a sense of purpose I had never experienced. Yes, it was all voluntary. Like me, the other Sunday school teachers were all professionals who held jobs during the week and stepped into Sunday school teaching mode on Sundays, and sometimes even Saturdays if there were special occasions to prepare for, which happened quite often in the Children's ministry. We were provided with a curriculum from the Diocese (Regional Church Mother body) with lesson plans to be followed to align with the Church liturgy. This was important, and as such, all the teachers were certified as lay ministers. I could spend endless hours on a Saturday afternoon going through the lesson plan and doing research, cross-checking, and referencing in preparation for the next day's class, an exercise I thoroughly enjoyed. It was during this phase that I discovered I had a knack for dissecting and uncovering hidden meaning, and most importantly, a gift for simplifying complex concepts for others. I got the most kick from how these young men and women's eyes beamed every time they grasped a concept, learnt a new skill, and when they completely understood the meaning in parables and a whole lot of other stories and lessons I would deliver. Our church's Sunday school was doing so well that I would get calls from other parishes asking me to come share what we were doing to achieve that, and I'd go conduct workshops to share. This part of my life spanned over 14 years until 2024, and it was the best period of my life, and I believe where a Blueprint for my purpose was revealed, as many elements of my calling surfaced here.

- **Element 1:** Teaching/Mentoring (Simplifying complex concepts).
- **Element 2:** Entrepreneurial/Visionary (Establishing a new curriculum/program).
- **Element 3:** Community Building (Attracting the "beyond Sunday school age").

However, it is the total state of flow I would find myself in that made it all worth it. Mihaly Csikszentmihalyi, a renowned psychologist, captures this state of being in the zone, the feeling of losing oneself in time whilst planning lessons or teaching all those skills, as Flow State—a peak mental state of complete absorption in an activity, characterized by deep enjoyment, total focus, creativity, and a distorted sense of time, where skills perfectly match high challenges. This lends scientific backing to the feelings of "pure joy" and "time vanishing" I was experiencing.

This chapter illustrates the **"green flags"** that signal one's true calling, often appearing in unexpected places after abandoning a misaligned path. These flags manifested as an innate desire for **autonomy** (starting the cleaning business), **excitement** and **industry exposure** (the Radio Frequency applications), and a profound sense of **joy and fulfilment** found in voluntary community work (the 14 years of Sunday school teaching and the creation of the Church University). The core discovery was a gift for **simplifying complex concepts** and **igniting understanding** in others, leading to a feeling of "flow."

1. **Look for the Flow State:** When time seems to **vanish,** and you are fully absorbed, you are in your "flow state"—the activity is directly aligned with your purpose.

2. **Joy over Check:** The highest signals of purpose often come from **voluntary activities** you would happily do for free, not necessarily from paid employment.

3. **Your Misfit is Your Signal:** Being a "misfit" or finding a professional environment "unhealthy" is not a personal fault but a strong signal of misalignment that demands a change in direction.

Part 2

Self-Discovery

Chapter 4:

Serendipity Mindset

Serendipity is often defined as a "fortunate accident". But it's not passive luck; it's an active mindset—the readiness to notice and capitalize on a chance opportunity. For me, Serendipity showed up as a new job delivering training, which felt like instant alignment. It showed up as a company needing a training associate. Yet, the greatest act of serendipity was the one I forced: *walking out*. When I stood up to my boss, I accidentally discovered the one thing my purpose required: absolute autonomy. This chapter is about how to stop fighting your desire for control and embrace the path of creative independence.

It was during the Sunday school teaching years, but in 2010, that my husband introduced me to a company looking for associates to deliver training to Business owners, executives, and HR managers on how to identify, acquire, and leverage talent within the workplace to enhance performance. This was a local office of an International Company with high standards and a strong reputation, so I was thoroughly trained and certified in the material and in how to deliver it. But somehow this came so naturally to me. I felt most alive when I was conducting training classes, which usually ran from 9-4 and lasted 3-5 days a week. I enjoyed delivering training and interacting with attendees; I revelled in this. Nothing gave me more joy than seeing them get their aha moments. Knowing that I had just illuminated someone, empowered them to go deal with an issue that was otherwise troubling them or stifling their business. Unfortunately, this phase of my career despite how much I loved it was short-lived, I think just over a year. You see, I was not a big fan of my boss's management style, and so it did not take long for me to stand up to her and eventually walk out, despite how aligned I felt in that role.

In hindsight, I realized that maybe I was just not suited to be an employee. I mean, I went on to work for two or so other companies, and even as a partner or shareholder with an executive position, involved in daily operations and management of others and with others, I would constantly want to do things differently, try new ways, be innovative, and that did not always sit well with most. At this one company, for a while, this one executive, the Managing Director, Chris, would disappear into any open door if he saw me coming down the hallway, just to avoid me lest I gave him another proposal, another suggestion, my opinion—God forbid. This got so bad that he got creative on how to avoid me. Chris's office had a filing cabinet that was just to the left of the door. And so, some days, I'd go to his's office to bounce some things off him, but on most days, I wouldn't find him. I'd know that he is on premises, but being a manufacturing company, I'd think to myself, he's probably on the factory floor. One day, through some odd twist, I discovered that no, in fact, Chris's in his office. On hearing my approaching footsteps, he'd quickly hide himself in the small space between the wall and the filing cabinet, and an open door would further block this off, and all I'd see in front of me would be an empty table, meanwhile he'd be to my left, hidden by the door. My presence clearly caused significant stress. He was also the type to shout at staff during performance meetings. Making people feel bad about their work contributions rather than trying to understand and see where he could help and motivate them. A different type of management style, I suppose, but it created that dreaded Monday morning tension in the office. The environment got too unhealthy for me, and as an executive, when I would try raise this with him… You guessed it, and so I felt muted and stifled. We eventually parted ways.

Endings as opportunities

Another sad realization, that even though one could be living out their purpose, a wrong vehicle (toxic work environment in this instance) can leave one feeling disillusioned. But my need for autonomy and innovation far outweighed the comfort of a title and a paycheck. The core idea was now to find alignment between one's inherent purpose and the path to take to express it in the world.

In Daniel Pink's book *Drive*: The Surprising Truth About What Motivates Us, Daniel argues that for complex, creative work, people are motivated by **Autonomy** (the desire to direct our own lives), **Mastery** (the urge to get better at something that matters), and **Purpose**. The whole chapter is a living illustration of this.

- **Our reliance, in organizations and schools, on a carrot-and-stick approach to motivation is outdated and often counterproductive.** We've long assumed that if-then rewards ("If you do this, then you get that") are the best way to motivate people. But decades of research show they can reduce performance, crush creativity, and dampen long-term motivation – especially for complex or creative tasks.

- **The three key elements in enduring motivation are autonomy, mastery, and purpose.** Autonomy is having a measure of control over what we do and how we do it. Mastery is making progress and getting better at something that matters. The purpose is to do something that makes a difference in the world or a contribution to others.

- **The most successful organizations are those that build environments where intrinsic motivation can thrive.** Companies that offer people control over their time, encourage continuous learning, and connect individual work to

51

a greater mission outperform those relying on rigid management and short-term incentives.

Chris was not necessarily a bad person, but the *system* was designed to punish innovation that came from outside the power structure. Autonomy and Innovative nature sometimes have no place in a traditional corporate structure.

"When You're Built to Lead the Dance."

Ask yourself, "Where are you currently hiding your own proposals?" "Who are you trying to avoid telling your next idea to?" "Why are you dimming your light?"

With all this drama, who needs employment, right?! In 2013, I resuscitated my business with renewed hope and energy, determined to do things my way, be innovative, and live out my dream of a new-age workplace. You remember the Telecommunication bug that had bitten me a few years back? I leaned into that. This time round, I started as a one-man band, "box dropping", buying IT equipment, adding a mark-up, and delivering to clients. This was slow and hard as I was not trained in IT, but I was free, which I valued the most. Initially, I did everything from learning product specifications, sourcing the product, writing proposals, collecting payments, making deliveries, and invoicing. It was long hours and sometimes sleepless nights. There were many costly learning curves, but I was not deterred. And over time, the business grew organically, largely because of my curiosity. "What if I could offer IT support with that? What about I introduce Network implementation and telephone systems?" I was constantly talking to clients and learning fast and was flexible and brave enough to expand in new directions. I learnt just enough to employ and bring in the relevant skills; the headcount increased, and our services expanded. We were now a player in the Telecommunication sector. The business grew, and even though we were classified as an SMME (Small, Micro, Medium Enterprise) by industry standards, we were doing fairly well. Enough to earn us some recognition in the industry. Within 7 years of operation, one got several accolades.

I remember like it was yesterday, the morning one of my employees arrived for work excited and shared with me that she had learnt on the radio that the National Small Business Chamber had opened nominations for the Woman in Business Awards, and that she had taken the liberty to nominate me. The news took me by surprise, but I was most grateful. What followed was a series of paperwork that one had to fill out as evidence of business operations and to capture the unique value of the business, its impact on employees, and its industry. Interviews and more paperwork later, we received the news that we had been shortlisted. I was beyond the moon with excitement and disbelief, "Was this really happening to me?"

The award ceremony date arrived, and naturally, my parents had to be there to witness this moment, and so it was great that we could extend the invitation. Walking into the awards venue, I was greeted by pictures of the nominees rotating on screens dotted around, and the glitz of the décor and spotlights were incredible. Being there with my husband and parents by my side made it even more special. The MC was great, witty, and funny, and this helped calm the nerves. I mean, there were several categories to go through and an incredible list of nominees, so of course I was nervous.

As the MC went through categories and winners were announced, we finally got to the category I was nominated for, and yes, my name was called, my face lit up, but my knees went jelly, and I swear my heart was pounding out of my rib cage. I remember lights flashing and the dramatic music as I made my way to the stage, all the while trying not to fall. Once the award was handed over, all I could think of was my mom. My eyes swept over the crowd and zoomed in on hers, and for a moment, everyone else and the noise disappeared as she smiled and nodded in affirmation. This was like my "Momma, I made it moment" moment. Her ability to spot my talents and the sacrifices she made to ensure she gave me the best possible foundation had all culminated in this. I know moms are always right, but if there ever was a moment mine could say that-- this was it! More awards and recognitions followed over the years, but this moment will forever be etched into my memory.

Awards and recognitions:

- 2015: The National Small Business Chamber-- Woman in business awards champion 2nd runner-up, in recognition of her efforts in business.
- 2017: Woman Entrepreneur of the Year Award finalist
- 2017: Entrepreneur of the Year finalist
- 2017: Regional Business Achievers Award Finalist

These were like stamps of approval, an affirmation that it was great I had listened to my hunch that I was not cut out to be an employee. All the fights, the struggles, and the going against the grain just meant I had something different to offer and had to be on my own to realize and achieve that. I felt validated.

Does that mean I set out chasing accolades? No! although I'll admit they were nice to have but at the heart of it, these were the results of pursuing what I felt passionate about. Proof that a life of purpose can lead to not only internal satisfaction but external rewards too. The lights and fanfare are short-lived and if one is not careful, one could be chasing the high to the detriment of one's own wellbeing, where purpose takes a back seat. Humans have a strong innate drive to compete— to be the best as compared to another, rooted in evolution for survival. Life is a competition; it would be folly not to think of it as such. We're constantly competing for resources, someone's attention, a promotion… it's a fact of life we can't escape and though its expression varies widely, it can be healthy or unhealthy depending on one's mindset and social conditioning. And awards can create a bottomless pit for external validations if you don't have the right mindset or don't have sight of what's important for the expression of your purpose.

The business continued to grow, and with that, my hunger to empower youth. And so, the company started offering learnerships, then internships, and, of course, employment upon successful completion of the courses. My passion for identifying and nurturing talent came through once again, and many youngsters with potential were absorbed and put to work on projects that would make most seasoned employees green with envy. Once again, I was happiest teaching and mentoring.

Chapter 4 establishes the concept of a **Serendipity Mindset**, which involves being receptive to chance opportunities and recognizing that resistance (like conflict with management) can be a signal. My experience in the corporate world, including a rewarding but short-lived training role and toxic executive positions (the "Carl's" story), revealed a fundamental truth: I required **Autonomy** to thrive. This realization led to the resuscitation of my business, which is focused on the Telecommunications industry. By leaning into my curiosity and **innovative nature**—constantly asking "What if I could offer..."—the business grew organically from a one-person operation to a recognized industry player, earning several accolades within seven years.

1. **Signs of Misalignment:** The intense frustration and tension experienced in traditional roles (like the conflict with Chris) are not character flaws, but powerful signals that your current environment lacks the **"what"** you need to fulfil your purpose.

2. **Serendipity is Active, Not Passive:** Purpose is found by being ready to act on chance opportunities (the "bug") and allowing your inherent curiosity to dictate the next step, rather than sticking rigidly to an old plan.

3. **Harness Your Strengths:** Your propensity for wanting to "do things differently" and "be innovative"—traits often penalized in rigid corporate structures—are the **exact elements** required to succeed when pursuing your own vision.

Chapter 5

The unlikely catalyst

I was already gone. Burnout had hollowed me out, and my exit strategy was three months from flawless execution. I planned to walk into the sunset, hand-delivering my successful Telecommunications company to the next generation of trusted leaders. The betrayal, when it hit, wasn't just a financial disaster; it was a physical shock that revealed a gaping hole in my life. It took an act of industrial espionage—a fire, theft, and a criminal case—to finally force me out of the game I needed to leave. That fateful Friday in September 2022 was not the end of the business but the beginning of my true purpose.

On Friday, my husband, who was now working for the same company, since it was now a family business, was working late at the office. I had already left as it was tradition that we knock off at 15:00 on a Friday, and besides, I was suffering from fatigue, in fact, burnout to be exact.

Burnout

We had just overcome several months of challenges in rolling out a Fibre Network in one of the Soweto townships, Protea Glen. Initially, this was a pride project, as at the time not many townships had Fibre for home Wi-Fi. And so, to be an Fibre Network Operator's implementation partner for such a project was quite a big deal. However, the challenges seemed insurmountable! Even though we thought we were prepared through engaging the community and local councillors prior to project start and going to the extent of employing labourers from locals and subcontracting to other smaller local companies, we still encountered acts of vandalism either to our equipment or vehicles, hooligans occasionally blocking roads, and at the height of it, arson. A fire attack on some of the sections where we had rolled out Fibre.

One of those attacks, I remember getting a call from a Protea Glen resident around 6 in the evening, alerting us that one manhole (a ground entry point for the fibre) was on fire. They had seen the office number from our installation vans, which were always in the area for this rollout. Anyone who has seen Fibre ducts knows they're plastic, and you can imagine the panic and scramble that ensues upon hearing this. The team that was nearby rushed to the said site, and of course, by the time they arrived, the fire had spread underground to other manholes. To say this was devastating is an understatement. All we could do was wait it out and report the incident. We had no suspect to pin this on. The witness saw nothing but smoke coming up from the manhole next to his house. The emotions that accompany such an incident are enough to send one to the hospital, and continuing to work in the very same environment can take a toll. This caused several project delays, stressful nights, and concerns about the safety of our staff and financial implications. It had been a lot to deal with, but by this time, things had settled down, and most glitches had been averted.

But I was finished, so done that I started planning my exit strategy. In fact, it was already underway. I had earmarked and started grooming one particular young lady to take over as MD of the company. She had joined the company several years earlier, along with many others, through a learnership programme, and had shown great potential. She was eager and hungry to learn. Always finishing her tasks ahead of time and keen to take on whatever else was available. She was one of those who were absorbed by the company after the learnership and rose through the ranks; at this point, she was the office manager. Still diligent, she understood the company's culture and espoused the spirit of what we were about. She was even helpful to others in other departments. Just the right candidate to take this company forward, I'd thought to myself. I began training her on all the other functions under my watch. I had so much trust that I gave her access to most systems. To test whether she could handle a task, I'd take a few days off and leave it to her. And true to character, she'd handle it with flying colours. As I grew more confident in her, I let go of most things and became comfortable. Parallel to this process, I had also been training the marketing manager and another young lady in the Tech department to do a bit more. Letting them liaise directly with our partners and clients, empowering them to solve problems where possible and to escalate only as a last resort. My plan was falling into place, and I had 3 months left before I could totally hand over and walk into the sunset. Or so I thought, until I got that call from my husband.

Betrayal

He called me from the office and told me to get dressed, as he was coming to pick me up for something he needed to show me back at the office. This was around 19:00. Of course, wondering what could be so important, I got dressed despite my state. He arrived, and we drove back to the office. On our way there, he started sharing what he had just discovered…

That day, he had a pressing proposal to finish, and hence he stayed late at the office. He thought everyone would be gone by 15:30, and he'd have no distractions and finish this proposal accordingly. Alas, that was not to be, as the MD candidate also hung around at the office much longer than usual. At some point, she asked him if he wasn't leaving as per Friday culture, but he just said he'd do so as soon as he was done. Several hours passed, and she was still there when my husband noticed she had started pacing up and down. This made him a bit uncomfortable, and his gut told him to stay put. This went on until it was nearly 18:00, and on noticing that not only was my husband not leaving but that her presence was starting to look suspicious, she decided to leave. A short while after she left, my husband decided to inspect the offices and found one desktop, the marketing manager's was still on. What he discovered on it was something none of us could ever have imagined. It was then that he decided I needed to get to the office right away.

When we got to the office, he led me to said laptop that had files that initially looked like my company but were shockingly dressed as something else. Then, traces of conversations, profile exchanges, different contacts, and banking details with our company partners. Evidence of several meetings that were attended with clients, but not under our company umbrella. Diarized marketing activities that were not on the company calendar, and in fact, one such activity was scheduled to take place that Saturday, the very next day from this, and hence, the office manager could not leave the office. She needed to load the marketing activation kit and all the other items they'd need for their planned activities. And now, I see you wondering "who _they_ are?"

Traces of the WhatsApp conversation, which was displayed on the marketing manager's desktop—"not smart", I hear you say —revealed a group of 5. Yes, four others were involved in this, and to make matters worse, they were all our employees. Three current and two had just left, hardly a month. Of the current employees, the Tech lady and the marketing manager were in on this. And so, three of the people I had been grooming and trusted to take over had literally taken over, just not in the way I had planned. They took everything I taught them, and I am using the word taught because 2 of the 3 had been with us since learnership programme many years prior, and everything they knew about this business, the skills and certifications they had acquired, they got here. And of course, the several months of mentoring into management functions as well. So yes, everything, and they used that, including our IP to try to establish their own company.

Now, don't get me wrong. I don't have anything against anyone starting a business. I did that, and it brought me such freedom and pleasure. But this, this was something else. It was obvious that the big 5 (I named them that since that moment) had decided to take over the business, dress it up as something else, and go off on their merry way, leaving me with nothing but a shell. Yes, they had registered a company with CIPC, used our company address, took our company profile as is and pasted it on their letterhead. They had contacted our partners and told them they're operating under a new name. They had meetings and got the new company boarded on our partners systems using our credentials, but new banking details, with the hope of diverting business to their new entity. They essentially stole all our Intellectual Property and trade secrets—all that using our resources. This seemed to have happened during working hours and right under our noses. The chunk of it, on days I'd be off, in an effort to test the office manager's capability and readiness to take over, and boy, did she not!

On discovering this, my body betrayed me — I shook uncontrollably, as though the ground itself was trembling beneath me. We spent endless hours in that office, clawing through files, unearthing fragments of betrayal, while my tears blurred the screen. Between the waters of grief and the snort on the keypad, I marveled bitterly at how the desktop did not collapse under the weight of my despair. Every minute that passed and with every document opened, I felt my hard work— a baby I built from nothing but grit and sweat, slipping through my fingers like sand. "Why? why would they do such a thing?! All I needed was a break!"

Now, after all the time and effort I had invested in this succession planning, I was never going to have that break; in fact, I now had a disaster on my hands. Grief and rage, raw and unfamiliar, consumed me whole. By the time we staggered out just after 10 p.m., my mind was a battlefield, thoughts racing with no mercy. And for the first time in my life, Monday — that ordinary promise of routine — felt too far, that I thought, "God, you have such a sense of humour, You reveal this to me on a Friday evening after everyone had gone home because You knew if it happened during working hours, I'd be in jail." I would have gone berserk on those 3. I was boiling with rage, but now I had 2 days to cool off and get my head right.

I used the rest of that weekend to gather all my facts, and on Monday morning, I got to the office for our usual Monday management meetings. I presented a slide deck of the newly formed company to all staff members. The culprits, sitting right there, and the look on their faces as they saw their company name and logo projected on the screen was priceless. I took my time and calmly presented this as if I were pitching a new company, its products and services, eventually closing with a contact details page and a snippet of the CIPC document with directors' details. That's when the penny dropped for the rest of the staff members who were not involved, and the three sat there, stealing looks at each other, sweating and uncomfortable in their chairs. Disciplinary hearing notices were issued against them, and they were all sent home immediately to prevent access to their workstations and to prevent tampering or deletion of evidence. As parallel to this, we had intended to lodge a criminal case.

I knew it was not going to be easy dealing with this, but honestly, I was not prepared for what followed. After the disciplinary proceedings concluded and the three were procedurally dismissed for their actions, they lodged a case of unfair dismissal with the CCMA (Commission for Conciliation, Mediation and Arbitration). This labour dispute resolution body aims to promote social fairness in the workplace. A well-known body that most employees turn to with their grievances. You can imagine my disbelief at this sheer display of disdain or perhaps naivety by these 3 when I received a notice from CCMA, but I had to go appear before them.

The days leading up to this were long and draining as I was also running from pillar to post trying to get the case lodged with the SAPS. (South African Police Service) The local branch police had no idea how to handle this matter. You see, this was not the type of theft where criminals are caught with a physical item, and the questions I was getting were, "Did the three take anything?" "Did they damage property?" Etc. I was made to explain this situation several times as one policeman would call another, then the second would call a third, and I ended up with a group of them all trying to figure out what charges to put on the sheet. Eventually, after what seemed like hours, one captain said he didn't see how they could assist. I can't even recall how I stumbled out of that police station — the world was a blur, my body moving on autopilot. But the moment I went through my kitchen door, the weight of it all crushed me. My knees buckled, and I collapsed, sobbing uncontrollably, drowning in a flood of tears. Then, without hesitation, my children rushed to me, wrapping me in a cocoon of arms — no judgment, no questions, only love. They held me as if their embrace could stitch together the fragments of the mother they had always known: the strong, unshakable "boss mom" now shattered before their eyes. And maybe, just maybe, their instinctive grip was not only keeping me from falling further apart but holding our entire world together.

Later that day, a friend called only to find me in that state of total collapse, still crying, that my words were unintelligible. I was gripped by a sense of helplessness, exacerbated by a deep, pre-existing burnout. My world was caving in, trusted employees had effectively stolen my company from under my nose, and with the police seemingly powerless to intervene, I lacked the emotional reserves to fight back. My friend listened patiently to my frantic explanation and, once I regained some semblance of composure, advised me to seek recourse through the commercial crimes court. Ah, with some glimmer of hope, I went looking for that court, and once there, I was advised to go to the Hawks.

- *The Directorate for Priority Crime Investigation (DPCI), commonly known as the Hawks, is the branch of the South African Police Service that investigates organised crime,*

> economic crime, corruption, and other serious crime referred
> to it by the President or another division of the police.

A captain at The Hawks' office assisted me. He listened to my story and guided me on which crime the three had committed. He helped with my statement and advised that I needed to take it back to the local police station to be lodged. Which I did, and only then was the matter enrolled, and an investigator allocated.

A few weeks later, I found myself at the CCMA to face the three. I arrived a few minutes before the set time and realized that only two had pitched. I greeted them, but they were having none of that. We quietly waited until we were called in. The CCMA councillor introduced herself and mentioned that she was a lawyer by training. She asked the complainants to introduce themselves and state their cases. After hearing their side, she did not spare them. She told them how shocked she was that they would even consider coming to the CCMA, as what they did was criminal and the CCMA could not help them in this regard. For the first time, they seemed to grasp the depth and seriousness of what they'd done.

Back at the office, the reality was that the company lost three staff members who were heading the departments of Admin, Marketing, and Tech. All the efforts invested in succession planning to help alleviate my workload had fallen flat, and at that point, I was in a far worse situation than when the plan started. Even though some staff members stepped up and were willing to take on the workload, which was highly appreciated, I couldn't see myself training and fast-tracking skills transfer; I just didn't have the energy. I was broken, suffering from anxiety, and I just could not face the world, let alone work.

After weeks of tears and not being able to get out of bed, I discussed handing over to my husband, and he agreed. In January 2023, three months after the ordeal, on the day we were supposed to return to the office for the new year, I sent a courtesy email to all my staff members informing them of my decision to resign. I set an indefinite out-of-office autoreply, and I switched my laptop off for good.

The days following that seemed long and unbearable. I could not get out of bed, let alone open the curtains. I lost all will to do anything. Apathy engulfed me, and I saw no way out. I was not looking for a way out. A phone ring would send my heart into palpitation mode that gave 4 cups of strong coffee a run for its money. I dreaded talking to anyone, and so I kept it off most of the time. I deleted WhatsApp and email apps from my mobile. I was done. I was too consumed by questions that I kept bouncing between self-blame and anger. "Where did it all go wrong? Why did I not see this coming? Why had I been I so trusting?"

"The Physical Toll of Misalignment."

I was never ready for the physical toll this ordeal had on me. I was already tired and on the verge of burnout, and the ordeal pushed me over the edge. This manifested in my body as fatigue, irritability, and insomnia. Despite being tired, it was impossible to shut down! I am not one to get sick easily, but now I was constantly suffering from flu symptoms, headaches, and lack of appetite. Not just for food but for going out and interacting, and the worst one, apathy! I was cynical and detached; I really couldn't be bothered even if you screamed "Jesus had just resurrected". Burnout steals your joy and turns you into a zombie.

The World Health Organization (WHO) officially classified Burnout as an occupational phenomenon that carries high emotional and physical costs for individuals, as well as substantial economic burdens for employers and society.

Prof Renata Schoeman, Head of Healthcare Leadership at Stellenbosch Business School, says burnout is a workplace phenomenon that cannot be confused with the daily stressors of everyday personal life responsibilities.

"Burnout is a persistent feeling of physical and emotional exhaustion that frequently comes with pessimism and disengagement from work. The culprits are usually an imbalance of resources and/or demands on what is expected of you at work versus the availability of time, finances, training, support systems, mentorship, and other resources needed for you to do your job."

"Another contributing factor is conflicting values: either a mismatch between your personal values and the organisational values, or the officially stated values of the organisation and the values in action."

The cost of burnout

Prof Schoeman further states that burnout can and should be avoided, but when it's left unmanaged, the monetary and non-monetary costs to the economy and businesses are unavoidably high.

Health economists estimate that unaddressed mental health conditions cost the South African economy **R161 billion per year** due to lost days of work, presenteeism (being at work but unwell), and premature mortality.

"The direct cost of burnout leads to increased absenteeism, reduced productivity, poor work performance, mistakes, and high employee turnover – all quantifiably impacting the organisation's bottom line."

"The hidden, indirect cost for businesses is the institutional loss of knowledge when employees leave, the time and cost spent on training and upskilling new employees, and the negative impact on organisational culture.

Prof Schoeman says the cost to the employee is their overall health and points out that burnout does not happen immediately but gradually builds over time, with subtle signs and symptoms.

"Although not a condition that is medically diagnosed, if left untreated, burnout can lead to mental health conditions that require medical treatment – this is not about simply taking a few weeks' holiday or resting to overcome the constant state of depletion."

Burnout contributes to depression, anxiety, and other stress-related disorders, impacting one's quality of living, relationships, and outlook on life. Physically, prolonged burnout can lead to cardiovascular disease, diabetes, gastrointestinal issues, and weakened immune systems."

Source: Stellenbosch University

https://www.stellenboschbusiness.ac.za/news/2024-07-01-real-costs-burnout-workplace

I spent what felt like an eternity wallowing in self-pity, until one morning in September 2023—exactly one year after the crash—when I realized I desperately needed sunlight and some fresh air. I ventured out for a walk through our estate in affluent Midrand. The experience was uncannily similar to my childhood walks from the bus stop to school; it felt as though a seed planted decades ago had finally manifested as my adult life.

Our complex featured a well-marked 3.5-kilometer trail, a serene path winding past water ponds teeming with ducks, majestic trees, and flowers that drew in a vibrant array of urban birds. On quiet mornings, the only sounds were the melodic birdsong and the gentle bubbling of water. Initially, I could only manage half the circuit—shocking for someone who's completed several Comrades marathons and so that should give you a sense of the depth of my despair, but with each passing week, my stamina grew until I could complete the full loop. I discovered a direct correlation between my mileage and my mood: as the kilometres added up, my spirit began to lift. I was slowly re-emerging into the world, though I remained far from ready to return to the demands of business. I lacked motivation and reason to go back. I had lost my fire. It took me a while to figure out what exactly was going on. Then, I made a realization that I could not trust anyone ever again in business, a big statement, I know, but I was just so broken. I even remember making a statement like, *"It would be so great to have a business where I didn't have to work with anybody"*. My dear husband would look at me lovingly and say, *"I don't think there's such a business."*

One thing that kept me sane through all this was church, not so much my faith but the UNI class, my service towards those kids. In hindsight, I realize that was purpose. Purpose is what kept me going. During same period I got nominated as Church Warden, a role which initially provided a much-needed sense of purpose, filling my desk with tasks that kept me focused and engaged. However, this respite was short-lived. As I delved into the role, I began identifying and challenging management practices that sat at odds with my principles. These confrontations strained the dynamics within the council, creating a palpable tension.

Only a year into my tenure, I chose not to seek re-election. I had seen enough; the transparency and integrity I expected had been replaced by disillusionment. Tragically, my perspective on the church shifted, regressing to the scepticism of my eleven-year-old self. With my faith in the institution fractured, I walked away.

Fortunately, this church departure coincided with our decision to sell our house and relocate. The move was driven by a dual purpose: practical downsizing as our children left for university, and a profound need to address my mental state following the business trauma. The daily walks I had been taking had crystallized a need for nature and distance from the relentless "hustle and bustle" of our town. I needed a serene environment to heal and rebuild. I had also taken up hiking, which my son had introduced me to in December of 2022 —three months after the ordeal. What had started as day hikes had escalated to multiday hikes that included camping out in the mountains under open skies. There's something soothing about being amongst trees, something cleansing about taking a dip in rock pools, something comforting in solitude.

I guess I had stumbled across a healing secret that the Japanese had long coined "forest bathing". The practice of immersing oneself in nature through all 5 senses to improve physical and mental health. If you've ever hiked, you probably have experienced it but did not think much of it. Well, there's something magical about moving slowly and aimlessly through a forest that the Japanese scientists have proven to be of some benefit like boosting the immune system, lowering cortisol levels and blood pressure, reduces anxiety, anger and fatigue. Try hiking next time you feel overwhelmed; go hug a tree, I highly recommend it. Besides we lead such "busy" lives. Have you ever noticed how frequently people respond with "I'm hectic" or "I'm so busy" when asked a simple "How are you?" In modern society, we have begun wearing "busyness" as a badge of honor. We proclaim our exhaustion with a strange sense of pride, as if the alternative—stillness or availability—would somehow diminish our worth or importance. But not at all.

When you pause from the chaotic noise of external stimuli and remove all the distractions albeit for a short while—you give your inner voice a chance to speak. There is wisdom in silence and if we are serious about being guided and getting clarity, we need to prioritise this. Be intentional about timeout and mindfulness, treat it like a high priority appointment, because it is.

The decision to move came at the right time because one morning, probably nearly 12 months after opening the criminal case, I received an SMS from SAPS, stating that the case had been closed for lack of evidence. Somehow, I had a sense that this was going to happen, as the case investigator had earlier indicated that the Prosecutor responsible for the case did not quite understand the charges. The captain at the Hawks had said it was Corporate Espionage, and this was stated in the statement. But upon receiving and reading the statement, the Prosecutor asked me to see him, and upon meeting with him, he suggested that he position it as cybercrime. It was not! and of course, naturally, there was no evidence to support that. I didn't have the energy or the will to fight, but instead I saw this as an opportunity to start afresh. A new beginning.

The Power of Rock Bottom

According to Post-Traumatic Growth (PTG) theory, the betrayal and burnout were necessary catalysts—a *precursor* to growth. PTG research suggests that profound psychological struggle can lead to positive change in relationships, priorities, and life views. PTG recognizes that the individual still experiences distress and psychological struggle; it is a process of positive change alongside the difficulty, not a replacement for it. And I can attest to this. I had gone through the pain, the depression, and had hit rock bottom, which ironically became a solid base from which to launch up. But I had to do the work, as active copying is key to overcoming this. This eventual shift to healing and new beginnings is a direct result of this trauma. Now I had a new perspective and appreciation for my resilience. I was once again excited about the possibilities that lie ahead.

What are your unlikely catalysts?

Who can forget Covid 19, a pandemic that had the whole world on its knees, not only from the illness that many lost their lives to, but also for the hard lockdown. A never-before-seen anomaly that had everyone locked up in their homes. Everything from shops, schools, places of worship, and workplaces was closed, with strict government instructions for everyone to stay home.

Something profound happened to many during this period; it was like a pause we never knew we needed. After the initial shock had passed and spring cleaning was done, the long days at home provided the much-needed time to reflect. Many took this opportunity to evaluate their health, marriages, relationships, homes, living conditions, and careers; none escaped this. A lot reported better physical and mental health as one of the benefits of that period. Some people's relationships suffered a blow, and others had an epiphany about their careers and did not want to return to their old jobs. Others used the time to learn new skills and start businesses.

This period dispelled many fears about work and careers. Could this have been an unlikely catalyst in your search for your purpose? Was that heartfelt side hustle the thing that kept you going through that uncertainty? Is it possible that you finally admitted that what your job was at the time was just a means of paying bills and not really fulfilling? The concept of working from home added another dynamic: people worked without supervision and realized they could manage themselves and their time profitably. Some realized they enjoyed autonomy and the flexibility it offered. Businesses had to adapt. It was never business as usual post that.

The BBC Future Forum research of 4,700 knowledge workers found that the majority never want to go back to the old way of working. Only 12% want to return to full-time office work, and 72% want a hybrid remote-office model moving forward.

Was it Covid, retrenchment? Ill-health perhaps? And did that eventually lead you to your purpose?

We don't always have to go through these traumatic experiences to get to this realization but unfortunately, many of us are too scared to leave our comfort zone to explore. But how comfortable really is the comfort zone?

This chapter details the **traumatic "unlikely catalyst"** that forced the me out of the Telecommunication business, a path I was already trying to leave due to burnout. While executing a succession plan, I was betrayed by trusted personnel who engaged in corporate espionage, using company resources and credentials to launch a rival firm. This betrayal, coupled with the frustration of the South African legal system's inability to handle the complex crime, resulted in overwhelming grief, anger, and anxiety. The profound emotional trauma forced me to resign and enter a state of deep **apathy and withdrawal**. However, this rock bottom ultimately served as the catalyst, forcing a radical geographical relocation and a break from the business world, paving the way for a new, self-directed chapter focused on nature and healing.

1. **The Crisis is the Catalyst:** When you ignore the small signals (fatigue, resistance), life often provides a crisis (betrayal, retrenchment) severe enough to **force the pivot** you were too afraid to make yourself.

2. **Burnout is a Physical Ultimatum:** Ignoring your purpose leads to severe physical and mental consequences (anxiety, apathy). Your body gives an

ultimatum when your mind refuses to change direction.

3. **Healing Requires Withdrawal:** Recovering from deep professional trauma requires a radical break—time in **solitude, nature, and detachment**—to regain mental clarity and the ability to trust oneself again.

Chapter 6

AHA moment.

I was the proud owner of five degrees in completely unrelated fields: Microbiology, Telecommunications, Business, Reiki, and now, Phytotherapy. What do these have in common? On the surface, nothing. In the quiet new town, nestled between rocky hills, I was just a woman puttering around, making body butters and herbal remedies. But this accumulation of knowledge—from science to spirituality—was my true 'Aha moment.'

Reflection and Re-evaluation

In December 2024, we arrived to take occupation of our new home and for me to start afresh in a new small town, a new neighbourhood, where I quickly learnt that regular coffee invites and check-ins were standard. We were warmly welcomed with home-baked treats and greeting notes from our neighbours Michelle and Manie, the kind of welcome I had only seen on TV. This generous gesture was shortly followed by another neighbour's Val. Regular coffee sessions, and waves from across the street became our new normal. The area itself was perfect, nestled between rocky hills, with lines of wattle trees on one side and a beautiful dam on the other. It was so serene I could finally breathe. I continued my morning walks in nature with my dog Spin, and I felt such a sense of peace. To be honest, I had little choice as Spin would literally be by my bedroom window every morning, looking in to see if I was coming out. There were days when he would not stop whining until I came out with his leash. He really can be a tough walking partner, but that kept me regular. On the business front, I had slowly gotten back but worked from home because the office was now far away, which suited me perfectly as I was still not ready to work with people. So, I handled bookkeeping and put in about 3 hours a day 3 or so times a week. The rest of the day I would fill with getting creative and experimenting with making body butters, cleaning detergents, and herbal remedies from natural ingredients, and my poor family had to be guinea pigs. All of a sudden, I was drawn to learning, and I enrolled for a whole lot of online short courses and studied at my own pace. The courses were in different fields, ranging from commerce to science, mysticism, and self-help. I would dedicate hours to my studies and later realized I had completed more courses in the natural sciences and self-help than any other fields. I seemed to have a natural disposition to those. I even got attuned and certified as a Reiki Energy Healing Practitioner.

Reiki is a Japanese form of energy healing based on the belief that a practitioner can channel a "life force energy" to promote relaxation and healing. A practitioner places their hands lightly on or just above a person's body to direct this energy, which is thought to help balance the body's energy flow and support the body's natural healing response.

The core principle in Reiki is that a person's energy flow ("ki") can become blocked by physical or emotional pain, leading to illness. Reiki aims to remove these blocks and improve the flow of energy. This helped me a lot during the healing phase because, in training which is taken live (not online), there was a strong emphasis on self-healing before healing others, which meant one had to practice on self first. Once attuned, I had to do an exercise in which I would lie in silence for about 60-90 minutes each day and practice Reiki Energy Healing on myself for 21 consecutive days.

Ultimately, the outcome of a treatment is still determined by the individual; but the most common outcomes are as follows:

- Relief of stress and pain
- Assists the body in detoxing
- Relaxes muscles
- Stimulates the immune system
- Assists in the feeling of being whole
- An increase in creativity
- An easier release of your emotions
- Increase in one's awareness
- The body's ability to heal is improved
- Clearing Energy blocks
- and an increase in energy levels

I also had to do daily journals of how the sessions made me feel for the duration of the 21 days. The first few days of the treatment were vicious. One got headache attacks, nausea, a running tummy, and a skin reaction. All of which are apparent ways the body purges. It wasn't easy, but one was determined to see it through, and quite frankly, it got better as the days progressed, and towards the last days, I started feeling a whole lot better. Energy levels increased, creativity soared, and I could handle my emotions better. I felt in control once again.

Thinking back, I realized I had been against the use of Western medicine for as long as I can remember. I don't know what informed that, call it intuition, but I had always been a natural cure/treatment option type of person if there was one available. I had been using onion to treat flu since my children were babies; in fact, they had never been to a doctor for seasonal flu or coughs. In my house, we often use everyday herbs from our garden and kitchen to treat various ailments or maintain good health and now, I had just added Reiki to my healing toolkit. Don't get me wrong, I appreciate the need for and importance of medical technology and there's a place for synthetic medication, but the list of side effects puts me off. This realization hit me hard when I found myself registered for a Master's in Phytotherapy. I could study for hours and often got lost in coursework and research. I cannot say why I was studying; I did not have a plan or a goal, but it was like therapy.

During this phase, I completed many of those courses and, a year later, earned a Master's in Phytotherapy.

> - *Phytotherapy is the use of plants and plant extracts to treat or prevent health conditions. It is a branch of complementary medicine that uses parts of plants, such as roots, leaves, and flowers, to make preparations such as teas, tinctures, and capsules. The therapeutic properties are attributed to the natural bioactive compounds, such as vitamins, minerals, and antioxidants, found in the plants. Source: World Health Organization (WHO)*

Now sitting here with all these academic qualifications and credentials, a Reiki attunement and a business I do not have a desire to go back to, one might ask, "What now?!" "What to do with all this?" What could my calling possibly be?

One thing became clear; self-realization requires self-education. You have to be hungry for knowledge but let your inner gps guide you so you equip yourself with complementary and relevant skills. Learning does not end "after school". If you're to prosper in this life, reinvention, curiosity and a teachable spirit are key traits.

Connecting Disparate Skills

This led me to the concept of Connecting Disparate Skills, that is, the ability to see links between seemingly unrelated disciplines or concepts. It became clear to me that pattern recognition and convergence of skills were key in fulfilling one's purpose.

This was further supported by the T-shaped professional concept, which state that A T-shaped professional is someone with deep expertise in one specific area (the vertical bar of the T) and broad, collaborative knowledge across several other disciplines (the horizontal bar), making them highly valuable for innovation, problem-solving, and adapting in complex, multidisciplinary environments by bridging gaps between specialists and seeing the big picture.

They combine specialized skills with generalist abilities, such as empathy, communication, and systems thinking.

The research gate

> *"T-shaped professional"-a metaphor for workers possessing both depth and breadth of skills and knowledge (Cotter, 2015; Harris, 2009). To visualize the "T-shaped professional," imagine the vertical line of a "T" representing a specific area of deep professional, disciplinary, and systems knowledge such as medicine along with a broader understanding (the horizontal line of the "T") of relational and cognitive skills that doctors connect to their deep knowledge such as emotional intelligence, empathy, presence, and communication skills. T-shaped professionals possess a repertoire of skills supporting collaboration and innovation with the other individuals and groups in their system (e.g., nurses and pharmacists)*
>
> *Source: The Research Gate*

Refilwe Marumo

If purpose is meant as a service to others' benefit, how do all the skills I've acquired serve others?

Qualifications	Skills	Needs addressed
Microbiology: Biological Science focused on the study of microorganisms (bacteria, viruses, fungi, etc.)	-Scientific Research -Analytical abilities	-Identifying disease causes. -Analysis.
Phytotherapy: A practice that uses plant-derived medicine to treat diseases	-Knowledge of alternative and natural ways to treat diseases. -Medicinal practice that leverages the pharmacological potential of plants.	-Treating ailments with herbal remedies. -Helping others with their health

Reiki: An alternative energy healing modality using universal energy (Ki)	Detecting energy blockages	-Treating ailments by activating the patient's body's natural healing abilities.
Business Management	Overall running of the business, including HR, Finance, and Operations	-Leader. -Mentoring others to reach their full potential
Telecoms MBA	-Technical problem-solving. -Critical thinking skills. -Soft skills like strategy and decision making	-Growing business and -bringing connectivity to others.
Sunday school teacher certificate	-Teaching skills	-Creating a curriculum. -Delivering lessons. -Imparting life skills.

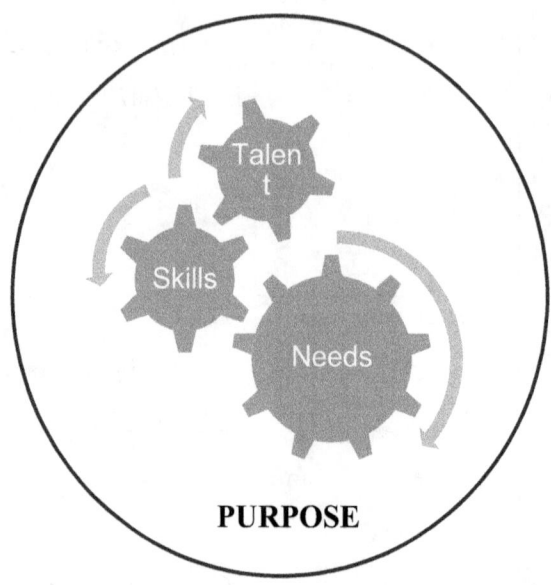

PURPOSE

My purpose was not in the corporate title or the lab coat. It was in the thread connecting everything that I was naturally drawn to: *the desire to simplify complexity, nurture talent, and facilitate healing.*

Purpose is often the intersection of multiple talents and different skills, not just one. And my T-stem is Science/Healing, and my crossbar is Business/Teaching.

Following the traumatic business exit, I found refuge and, healing in a new, quiet town, embracing solitude and nature walks. This period of withdrawal acted as a psychological incubator, allowing an innate curiosity to surface. I began accumulating knowledge through courses, naturally leaning toward Natural Sciences, herbal medicine, and energy healing (Reiki), This chapter defines the "Aha Moment" as the realization that purpose lies in the convergence of seemingly disparate skills and passions— In my case, scientific rigor, business management, and an innate drive to simplify complex concepts and facilitate healing—all pointing toward a life dedicated to holistic well-being.

1. **Look Back for Clues:** Your "Aha Moment" often isn't a flash of new inspiration, but the **sudden realization of a pattern** that has been present in your life since childhood.

2. **Inner work is vital:** the process of reflection and healing is an important step toward moving past trauma to reach your new beginning. You cannot move forward with old baggage.

3. **All Skills Converge:** No knowledge is wasted. Purpose often lies in the **intersection** of seemingly unrelated skills (e.g., combining a science degree with teaching skills for healing).

4. **Joy is the Ultimate Metric:** The activities you can spend hours on, losing track of time (studying, experimenting, creating), are the ultimate **"green flags"** confirming the direction of your calling.

Part 3

Realising your Purpose

Chapter 7

Putting together the pieces of the puzzle

At this point, it looked like life had just presented me with pieces of a puzzle, perhaps even multiple puzzles, as nothing was making sense. Were these four separate lives, or were they pieces of a single puzzle? After the crash, I yearned for a SOUL-ALIGNED profession—one free of staff and corporate chaos. But I was stuck, paralyzed by the sheer volume of my own experience.

Despite the clarity of my intentions, I found myself at a professional crossroads, struggling to synthesize these disparate elements into a cohesive path forward. The very notion of a "next pursuit" felt paradoxical; after all, I was the same individual who, amidst the volatility of my crash, had resolutely declared my intention to take early retirement. I began to wonder if this newfound restlessness was a sign of healing—a signal that my professional mission was not yet concluded. Perhaps I was merely transitioning to a higher level of operation. However, clarity remained elusive.

While I knew with absolute certainty that I would not return to the telecommunications sector, I lacked a definitive roadmap for what lay ahead.

My primary internal mandate was clear, if unconventional: I sought a model that required no personnel management and bypassed the traditional constraints of a 9-to-5 structure, regardless of ownership. While "avoidance" is rarely a robust career driver, I was yearning for a vocation that resonated with my core values and inherent gifts—a space where I could operate with total authenticity while delivering meaningful impact.

In recent years, I had turned to journaling as a way to pour my thoughts out onto paper. It got me through my ordeal. It was good for my mental health. As part of my healing journey, together with walking, breathwork, and meditating, I also noticed that I started seeing a lot of repeating numbers. This started randomly with numbers like 1111, 444 seemingly appearing on random things like the car dashboard, the kilometre reader, the clock, the time on the laptop, registration numbers, and so forth. After several months of this happening, I got curious and started researching. I discovered that these were called Angel Numbers and that they carried messages, I suppose for those who believe in that sort of thing. And so, I started taking note of these synchronicities, and I would journal daily all the numbers I had seen, and in the evenings, I'd look up their corresponding meanings. I remember one particular day when I had been taking my usual morning walks and got home to make coffee. As I was standing by the microwave, I noticed 09:09. I had been seeing this for several days, and so I turned to Google to find the meaning behind this angle number. The uncovered meaning not only gave me hope but also led me to explore other numerological phenomena, such as life path numbers.

The angel number 0909 is a powerful sign of spiritual growth, signifying a period of completion, spiritual awakening, and new beginnings. It suggests a major life transition is underway, encouraging you to align with higher spiritual energies and trust that you are on the right path. The number combines the infinite potential and spirituality of the number 0 with the completion and humanitarianism of the number 9.

Life Path Numbers

I was now intrigued. The universe had my attention, and one thing led to another. I came across life path numbers and delved a bit more into these, too.

> *Life path numbers are a core concept in numerology, derived from a person's birth date to reveal aspects of their personality, destiny, and life journey.* See **table 7.1 hereunder.**

Meanings of the Life Path Numbers

A person's birthdate digits (day, month and full year) are summed up and reduced to just one number. Each number carries a unique energy and sets of traits as per this table.

Life Path Number	Key Traits	Challenges
1	Natural leader, independent, ambitious, innovative.	Can be bossy, overly assertive, or struggle with accepting criticism.

2	Diplomat, sensitive, cooperative, intuitive, aims for harmony.	Can be conflict-averse, overly dependent, or seek external validation.
3	Creative, expressive, charming, optimistic, and a communicator.	May struggle with discipline, focus, or creating drama.
4	Practical, hardworking, reliable, organized, and seeks stability.	Can be rigid, stubborn, or needs to learn flexibility and take risks.
5	Adventurer, free-thinking, adaptable, curious, progressive.	Can be restless, impulsive, or struggle with commitment and daily responsibilities.
6	Nurturer, responsible, compassionate,	Tends to overextend themselves, be controlling, or

	family-oriented, healer.	have difficulty setting boundaries.
7	Seeker, analytical, introspective, spiritual, intuitive.	Can be secretive, distrustful of others, or prone to perfectionism.
8	Achiever, ambitious, goal-oriented, natural leader, focused on abundance.	Potential for being a workaholic, controlling, or balancing material with emotional needs.
9	Humanitarian, compassionate, idealistic, old soul, visionary.	Can struggle with letting go of the past or transcending day-to-day life.
11	Intuitive, visionary, inspiring, spiritual enlightenment.	High pressure, deep life lessons, potential for being overly sensitive or impractical.

| 22 | Master Builder, practical idealist, capable of large-scale success. | Requires immense effort and focus. Challenges can be intense. |
| 33 | Master Teacher, focused on unconditional love, higher consciousness, and empathy. | High level of responsibility and self-awareness required to embody its potential. |

Table 7.1

After adding my birthdate digits together, I discovered I was a Life Path 7, see the table above for meaning. Intrigued by all this, I kept researching, delved deeper, and discovered what is known as The Core Blueprint, made up of two extra pillars--Soul Urge and Destiny Expression, over and above the life path number. The Core Blueprint provides a holistic view of a person's character and purpose in life, derived from their full birth name and birth date. This blueprint is thought to map out key aspects of an individual's life journey and potential. Through that, I quickly learned that I'm also a Soul Urge 9 (meaning: inner yearning helping humanity at large, a genuine responsibility to change the life of others) and a Destiny Expression 8 (meaning: an illuminator, mastering the material world, leader)

Now armed with all this new information, it was like my eyes had suddenly been opened. What does all this mean? I was bubbling with excitement. For the first time in a very long time, I saw light at the end of the tunnel.

According to this Core Blueprint a person with a **Life path 7** displays the following traits:

- They are a mirror of consciousness.
- Here to uncover, articulate, and transmit hidden truths, transmitting knowledge into wisdom that liberates others. (the illuminator/teacher/healer)
- Their ultimate purpose is to bridge intellect and spirit, making understanding itself a healing act.
- needs solitude to recharge

Soul Urge 9:

They feel profound connection to all of humanity.

- Natural teacher, Consellor or spiritual guide

- Has innate wisdom

- Creative expression such as writing to communicate

(*CAN YOU BELIEVE THIS*)

Destiny Expression 8:

- Possesses natural authority

- Resilience and ability to overcome setbacks

- The one who turns abstract ideas into tangible results.

- Ability to assess people's strengths and weaknesses

- Leader who uses power to implement truth and healing.

To establish the accuracy of this, I tried it on these two well-known personalities

1. Nelson Mandela: 18 July 1918

Calculation: $1+8+7+1+9+1+8=35$

Further reduce to single digit: $3+5=8$

Meaning: Number 8 is the number of **leadership, power, and authority**. It signifies a person capable of building something lasting and influential, often requiring great resilience and self-discipline.

2. Oprah Winfrey: 29 January 1954

2+9+1+1+9+5+4=31

Reduce further to single digit: 4

The core blueprint for numerology number 4 centers on **stability, structure, hard work, and practicality.** Individuals with a strong 4 influence (such as a Life Path or Expression Number 4) are known as the "Builders" focused on creating secure foundations in all areas of life.

You can decide for yourself if this exercise is worth doing but I thought there was something there. Like the saying goes: It is written in the stars. What if numerology holds the answers? The concept comes from ancient astrology, where people believed that the position of celestial bodies at birth dictated destiny, implying that life events are predestined by a cosmic plan or similar to the religious interpretation of it "Gospel in the stars" a theory of a divine message encoded in constellation.

The analytical power of intuitive systems

But all these coincidences and synchronicities, mysterious as they might have been, could be explained. Have you ever thought of someone intensely, and right at that moment, your phone rings, only to be them calling you? Or you have a particular issue you've been grappling with, and all of a sudden, someone out of nowhere talks to that issue. This actually happened to me a lot recently when I was procrastinating writing this book and decided to go to the shops instead. As soon as I got into the car to drive off, a song titled Unwritten by Natasha Bedingfield started playing. Needless to say, I got the message, loud and clear and you'd know what I mean if you know the lyrics to this song. Or like when my neighbour invited me over for coffee, only to gift me a brand-new book she had helped type-set, and the time a friend invited me to a book launch when I was battling to finish mine. There's apparently an explanation for all those episodes. Modern society might attribute this to being signs from a higher power or consciousness, and sceptics might explain it as seeing what you're subconsciously looking for. Carl Jung's concept of synchronicity, which explains how to recognize signs from the universe and their meanings, does so beautifully. When two or more events happen simultaneously that are related in meaning but do not cause one another, the internal psychic mirrors the external events and thereby provides confirmation, direction, or a sense of alignment to the recipient.

Carl Jung's concept of synchronicity describes **meaningful coincidences** *where an inner psychological state (thought, dream, feeling) aligns with an external event, seemingly without a causal link, suggesting a deeper connection between mind and world, an "acausal connecting principle. It's about events that are not random but feel deeply significant, often offering guidance or insight, linking the inner psychic world with the outer material world in a meaningful*
pattern. https://www.psychologytoday.com/za/basics/synchronicity

The appearance of angel numbers, synchronicities, and numerology was not a mere coincidence; these were meaningful tools that served psychological development, thereby giving credence to my self-discovery journey. Was I being guided?

Finding the Common Thread

Ask yourself:

- What do you lean towards the most, despite the many skills you may have?
- What problems are you drawn to solving?

Use Table 7.2 as an example to help you map out your qualification, skills and links to your Core blueprint.

- o **Microbiology/Phytotherapy:** Deep Scientific Basis with a focus on Natural Healing.
- o **Telecommunications/Business:** Leadership, Systems Management, and Problem Solving.
- o **Sunday School Teaching/Reiki:** Simplifying concepts and Directing Energy for Change.

Qualifications	Skills	Links to Core Blueprint
Microbiology: Biological Science focused on the study of microorganisms (bacteria, viruses, fungi, etc.)	-Research and -Identifying disease causes	-Healer. -Drawn to understanding the invisible
Phytotherapy: A practice that uses plant-derived medicine to treat diseases	-Knowledge of alternative and natural ways to treat diseases -Medicinal practice that leverages the pharmacological potential of plants.	-Healer -Enlightener transmitting knowledge into wisdom that liberates others.
Reiki: An alternative energy healing modality	-Detecting energy blockages -Treating ailments by activating the patient's	-Healer

using universal energy (Ki)	body's natural healing abilities	-Mystic scientist of the soul
Business Management	-Overall running of the business, including HR, Finance, and Operations	-Leader -Mentor
Telecoms MBA	-Technical problem-solving, -Critical thinking skills. -Soft skills like strategy and decision-making	-Leader -Articulates knowledge into wisdom
Sunday school teacher certificate	-Creating a curriculum -Delivering lessons	-Creative/ Creator -Teacher -Spiritual messenger

Table 7.2

The Common Thread suggests that my purpose is to use my **scientific rigor** (Microbiology/Phyto) and **communication skills** (Teaching/Training) to empower

116

people toward **holistic well-being** (Reiki/Herbalism). This is my unique value proposition.

My pieces of the puzzle suddenly seemed useful. I could connect the dots that aligned with all this, there were lots, and these findings resonated. Of course! Instantly, I felt like I had hit life's biggest Powerball jackpot! It wasn't until I traded the logical spreadsheets for the unseen language of numbers that the scattered pieces—the seeker, the scientist, the teacher, the healer—finally locked into place.

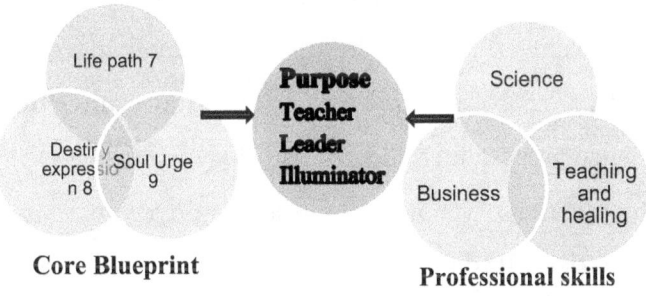

Core Blueprint　　　　**Professional skills**

It was through this decisive turning point from trauma and apathy to renewed direction, driven by the desire for a Soul-Aligned Profession free from people management, that I began my internal search through journaling and found meaning in the appearance of Angel Numbers and subsequently Numerology. By calculating my Life Path 7 (Seeker/Analytical), Soul Urge 9 (Innate wisdom, humanitarian), and Destiny Expression 8 (Leader), I found the unifying framework for my disparate experiences (science, business, teaching, and healing). The excitement of realizing that my purpose lies in empowering others uncover their internal truths for healing and self-actualization confirmed my readiness for a new, mission-driven chapter.

1. **Look for the Unifying Blueprint:** Purpose often requires moving beyond conventional career analysis to use **intuitive or spiritual frameworks** (such as numerology or astrology) to discover the inherent psychological needs that drive you.
2. **Crises Redefine Values:** The trauma of burnout and betrayal clarified the non-negotiable career drivers: **autonomy, solitude, and strong impact**, proving that deep dissatisfaction is a precise map of what you need.

3. **The Pieces Were Never Random:** Every major pursuit——was unconsciously driven by the core blueprint, validating that seemingly random decisions were actually **preparatory steps** for my ultimate calling.

Chapter 8:

Battling Resistance

The realization of your purpose is a high, an intoxicating mix of relief and certainty. For me, it was a few blissful days walking on cloud nine. But purpose is not a destination; it's a commitment, and the moment you decide to act, it seems the honeymoon is over. That's when the gatekeepers of your comfort zone—**Fear, Doubt, and Imposter Syndrome**—come knocking. Discovering your calling is the easy part. The battle is what happens next. In this chapter, we equip ourselves with the basic tools needed to move from blinding realization to tangible action.

Writing this very book was a first and conscious effort to live out my purpose, but it presented challenges; I had many a moment of resistance. "What do I even have to offer?" "Why would anyone be interested in my story?" This made the early days of writing rather difficult. I would procrastinate, find other things to do, and leave it for days.

Psychological Barriers

Steven Pressfield's *The War of Art* tackles this issue of psychological barriers quite well. This book is the definitive text on **Resistance**, exactly what I was experiencing. The negative, internal force that prevents creative work. It made sense that my fear, doubt, and procrastination were not personal failings, but rather a universal force that attacks those nearing their true calling. Powerful conceptual tool for naming the enemy.

"How many of us have had a great idea and felt the rush to action it, only to take the first step, and stop dead after that?" A classic example is the New Year's resolution syndrome. You set a goal to be fit and healthy for the New Year and sign up for a gym membership to prove your seriousness. Come the first week of January, the gyms are overflowing with eager new members on a mission, and you're one of them. You are committed to a healthy lifestyle, you see yourself in a bikini, and you probably have already bought it; one or two sizes smaller, as motivation. Only to drop out a few weeks later with all sorts of excuses. *"Work got busy. "Traffic in the morning is impossible; besides, I'm actually not in that bad of a shape,"* and the bikini and monthly debit orders become a haunting memory of a dream unrealized.

It is important to realize that limiting beliefs work quietly in the background, shaping decisions and plans. Without clear awareness, they can cause hesitation, second-guessing, and a lack of confidence that can slow or stop progress. This internal resistance may manifest as procrastination or self-sabotage, making it harder to follow through on goals aligned with your values. Because these beliefs feel so natural, you might never question them unless you take time to reflect intentionally. When you begin to examine the source of your doubts, you can understand how they block fulfilment and how overcoming them opens new opportunities for personal direction and satisfaction. This process involves shifting perspective from *"I can't"* to *"What if I could?"*—a powerful shift in mindset that leads to growth.

> *Most of us have two lives. The life we live and the unlived life within us. Between the two stands resistance.*
>
> —Steven Pressfield

It became apparent to me that finding one's purpose is not immune to resistance, and I was not unique. In today's modern world there's no shortage of disturbances and distractions all vying for our attention, all contending to get our focus, one trying to be more noticeable than the other. We juggle so many different balls and whether we're winning at this or not, somehow, we convince ourselves that it is possible. But when one more ball is thrown into this, an important one at that, like nurturing one's purpose, then procrastination and all distractions come flooding in; I was suffering from mental forces, but now I could name the enemy. The story needed to be out, and I was just a conduit. Looking at it, this way helped dissolve much of the resistance. Instead of excuses, I put measures in place. I committed 3 hours per day to writing. My phone would be off, and I would limit distractions as much as possible

123

during those hours, only getting up for bathroom breaks. And then I reached a sweet spot; once I tapped in, I could not tap out. There were nights when, despite how tired I was, I just couldn't fall asleep. The lines would keep coming, and it felt like the book was literally pouring out of me. Mornings couldn't come fast enough, and I would find myself grabbing a bedside notepad, trying to catch up with this flow. Procrastination and distractions are synonymous with modern day life but aligning oneself to the vital quality of being focused is important if we're to thrive in our endeavours. So establish boundaries, set deadlines and push through obstacles and there will be many, but persist. It turns out, distractions are like little bullies, they scuttle the minute you stand up to them, they disappear when you knuckle down.

Imposter Syndrome

I mentioned earlier in one of the chapters that it was only when I engaged in activities outside academics that I discovered I have other talents. Since my 20s, I've often been asked to host friends' baby showers. I got asked to MC at events. I got to be the assigned creative at parties and high teas, to give speeches at family functions, and so on. All of which pointed to my talents, and it could have hit me in the head many times, but I wouldn't have seen it at the time. Now thinking about it, I enjoyed fulfilling all those. I would ask the host for the theme or intention of the event and often did not mind taking time before the date to research, write speeches, and prepare for them. I always felt good standing in front of crowds sharing what I had learnt. The speeches would be event-appropriate, light but informative. Fun if the occasion called for it but always had some takeaways. I often had attendees come up to me during tea or after the event to compliment me on the task I had just delivered, and some wanted to delve deeper into what I had just said. All signs pointed to the fact that I was clearly gifted with good communication skills, but it never crossed my mind that I could pursue a profession in line with all this. I always felt I was just a friend helping out, not a professional speaker who could charge fees for this, but this is a classic example of "Imposter syndrome," The feeling that you'd be a fraud if you charged fees despite external evidence of competence. How many times has someone called on you for a "small favour?" a quick opinion or to pique your brain?

If you take the time to think about it, you might realize that that's because you're pretty good at that one thing and then take it a step further; hone it sharply and it could just lead to a consultancy business.

The Entrepreneurial myth

Another myth is that most people think some things are just passions and never consider them viable business opportunities or income generators. Let's face it, we all have bills to pay, and month-end comes around faster than you can say "debit orders," and so a fear of starting on your own is mostly a fear of having no income, and it is real! And it has stopped many dreams in their infancy, but there are ways, and some have had breakthroughs.

I have a cousin, Tebogo who is a good cook. She was often drawn to work involving food, so worked in the deli sections of FMCG retail outlets for most of her life. At some point, she lost her job and was home for a while, and we all know how tough that can be. As usual, one searches for a new job and sends their CV to different companies in the hope of finding related or experience-based work. But this did not yield results quickly enough, and after years of struggle, my cousin, now in her mid-40s, slowly and accidentally got into cooking for small events. She'd always been in charge of food at family functions. She always got compliments on her food because it's tasty. She could make food taste good and consistent, whether she cooked for 5 or 500 people. And so, it was only natural that she packaged this and offered it as a service. She overcame a limiting belief that she needed to be employed; she acknowledged that she had a gift, was passionate about food, and could realize her purpose in cooking on her own, and she started pursuing it. She now offers catering services for all sorts of events, from funerals (and we all know how big black funerals can be), birthdays, special occasions, and so forth. Now that she was fully in, she began to see other opportunities within that space. She went on to invest in décor so she could offer a total package and thereby expanding her offering. She is happiest cooking and now even more so as she can get creative through her own catering and events company. She is always booked; her business is spreading mostly through word of mouth.

She never complains about the magnitude of events, the long hours, difficult clients, or unreliable suppliers. Challenges are there, but she seems to be handling them rather well; she seems to have boundless energy, and you can just see that she truly is happy. Her calling is to feed people, and that has become a source of income. A big contrast between her old job in the deli section where she followed rules and her new catering business where she creates *flavour* emphasizes the difference between doing food work and living a food purpose.

So, look at every avenue, not just work. On the social side, what are your friends and family often saying? Look for clues.

- What activities are you drawn to?
- What gaps do you often identify?
- What do you seem to always come up with solutions for?

See if you can identify patterns.

Chapter 8 examines the intense **Resistance** that follows the spiritual euphoria of purpose discovery. While initial relief and certainty are present, the realization that **immediate tangible action is required triggers fear, doubt, and Impostor Syndrome**. The chapter addresses this battle by providing tools to recognize latent talents. Historical clues (frequent requests to MC, host, and speak) that I previously dismissed as mere "favours." And through the case study of my cousin, the caterer, the chapter debunks the myth that **passions** cannot be **viable, soul-aligned professions**. It encourages the reader to look beyond conventional work structures to the patterns found in social life, compliments, and problem-solving instincts.

1. **Resistance is Proof:** The presence of intense fear and doubt (Resistance) is a sign that you are on the brink of **meaningful, soul-aligned action**, and should be treated as a validation, not a deterrent.

2. **External Validation is a Clue:** Your purpose is often hidden in plain sight, found in the **consistent requests and compliments** you receive from

friends and family—the things others rely on you for and that you perform effortlessly.

3. **The Passion vs. Profession Myth:** Relegating your passion (like cooking or speaking) to a hobby is a limiting belief. A purpose-driven life merges the two, channelling **boundless energy** into overcoming challenges that align with your calling.

Chapter 9 Conclusion:

The Unstoppable Calling

One practical step to start distinguishing between career and life purpose is to ask yourself what drives your decisions: Are you motivated by external rewards like money and status, or by internal rewards like passion and impact?

Understanding your true motivations clarifies where your focus should lie and how to allocate time and effort. This clarity can lead to more deliberate choices, whether that means developing new skills, changing careers, or deepening personal commitments outside work.

The journey we've taken together, moving from the restrictive comfort of the societal mould to the chaos of the catalyst, and finally to the quiet certainty of your authentic calling, confirms one essential truth:

You are not here to live someone else's gospel.

The Act of Emancipation

Finding one's purpose or calling is indeed just the first step. The true transformation lies in the second step: Action! That action begins with an act of emancipation—you must strip away the expectations and the pre-conceived identity others have placed on you, but most importantly, the identity you have clung to for years.

For me, the painful truth revealed by the "unlikely catalyst" was the immense pressure of trying to sustain the identity of a **"businesswoman"** I was suffering needlessly by observing that limiting description. There's nothing wrong with professional labels or titles, except, one needs to peel the layers off and get to the heart of what it is that you're doing under that "hat". How is it of service to others? Hindsight and deep reflection showed me that my value was never in the degrees, title, or the revenue; it was in the underlying **processes and principles** that I brought to every role, underpinned by my authentic and innate talents:

- **Simplification:** Always striving to distil complex processes into clear, manageable steps.

- **Engagement:** Identifying people's strengths and fostering environments where they felt safe to contribute and thrive.

- **Challenge:** Consistently questioning the status quo to build healthier systems and culture.

Whatever role I was holding, my core functions were always the same: creative problem-solving, system improvement, and human development.

Talent, skill, and purpose connection

Most of the time, it takes others to point out your talents, like how early on my mother realized I had potential, which prompted her to move me to an environment that would nurture it. (chapter 1)

Similarly, my election as Prefect and subsequently as Deputy Head Girl indicates that others recognized my leadership talent. However, that did not stop there; skills development was provided to enhance it (Chapter 6 leadership camp).

This is further demonstrated later, when I started a business with nothing but guts and later had to enrol for a postgrad in Business Management because I noticed I lacked the skills to succeed.

How I volunteered to teach Sunday School despite walking out of church at age 11. I was not a teacher in a formal sense, but training was provided, and after a few teaching sessions, my talent emerged and shone through. All this demonstrates that Purpose has the power to expose and channel your talents in the right direction and inform what skills you will need to carry out your mission, if you just tune in.

Summary of the 5 steps to discovering your purpose

1. Make a list of your talents, the skills you have acquired, and hobbies.

Identifying personal purpose involves introspection and honest self-evaluation. Start by reflecting on moments when you felt truly fulfilled. Consider the activities that excited you or the challenges that fuelled your passion. These experiences often point to underlying values and interests that can help shape your purpose. Keeping a journal can be an effective way to capture these reflections over time. Write down what you enjoy, your skill, and what you aspire to achieve. This exercise not only clarifies thoughts but also provides insights into the recurrent themes that resonate with you.

Talents: Tools to fulfil your purpose	Skills: Enhance your talents	Hobbies
-Natural ability -Aptitude	-Taught -Acquired through deliberate effort -Training and practise	-What you enjoy -Activities you spend time on

2. The green flags detection system

Engaging in discussions about your aspirations and dreams can spark deeper reflection on your purpose. It is also important to remember that finding purpose does not have to be a solitary journey; sharing ideas with others can provide motivation and inspiration. Joining groups or communities focused on personal development can yield valuable insights and connections.

Use the green flags to counter the "Imposter Syndrome" discussed in Chapter 8.

- **The Internal Signal (The Flow State):** The tasks where you lose track of time (Chapter 6).

- **The External Signal (The Compliments):** The talents that people constantly ask you for and validate (Chapter 8).

- **The Historical Signal (The Common Thread):** The underlying principle present across all your jobs (Chapter 6).

3. Find your Core Blueprint

Using Numerology to establish your life path numbers (life's journey and purpose), and Destiny/Expression numbers (talents and potential shared in Chapter 7).

These numbers, along with others such as the Soul Urge (inner desires) and the Personality (outer self), form a map that reveals your innate strengths, challenges, goals, and personality traits, providing self-awareness and guidance for your life's path.

Follow the example in the resource page to calculate yours using your birthdate and full name

You can use a free online Core Blueprint calculator for this. Prompt like this: factor in your full name and birthdate into the search bar and ask- "calculate my life path and follow with Core Blueprint"

4. The Universal Common Thread

The most powerful lesson of this book is that your purpose is not a mystery, but a **universal common thread** linking every major life event, skill, and talent. In my journey and in yours, purpose lies at the intersection of three critical domains—talent, skills, and world needs. A concept often known as **Ikigai.** But your unique purpose map (your core blueprint), takes this even further by exploring how you can use these to inform your career choice and make a living. Ideally, the main reason for finding your purpose is to make a living that feels aligned with your core values. To limit the unpleasantness of doing work you hate just for the sake of money. We learnt earlier that that is unsustainable and leads to burnout and other health issues. Aligning one's purpose with Profession is the sweet spot we all should strive for. 5. The Goal is a SOUL-ALIGNED profession.

- **Your Who? (Core Blueprint+ Hobbies):** *Example: Example: teaching/mentoring, healing, solitude, nature.*

- **Your How? (Skills):** *that you acquired either through structured learning or experience Example: Scientific rigor, simplifying complexity.*

- **Your Why? (Mission):** This is most important as it's your reason for being. Your mission in this life *Example: Healing, enlightenment, serving/ being of service.*

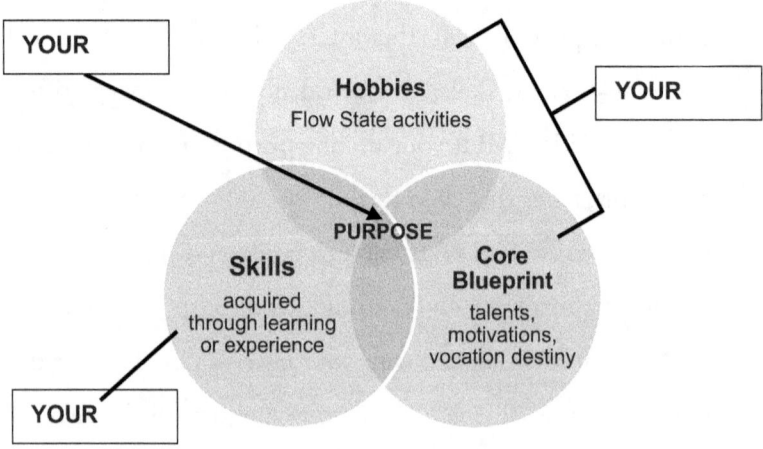

The Purpose Diagram

5.Formulate your Purpose Statement:

When you find the overlap of these areas—Your PURPOSE, **you're able to search for and find work that aligns with your gifts, meet the world's need and sustain you**—you find unstoppable alignment."

Whether you believe in the analytical tools of **numerology** (Chapter 7), the gentle nudges of **angel numbers**, or the dramatic shock of **catastrophic events** (Chapter 5), be on the lookout. Life always provides hints. The challenge is that we are often too busy chasing *external* validation to hear the *internal* whisper.

By putting together, the pieces of my multi-faceted puzzle, the core purpose became undeniable:

- I provide environments that encourage **exploration and deep, conducive learning**.
- I mentor, help, and guide people towards **development and enlightenment**.
- I challenge the status quo and pose questions that make others **think things through**.

- I use both the **scientific method and spiritual intuition** (Phytotherapy and Reiki) to bridge intellect with spirit.

I am a **teacher, a healer, and an enlightener**. In whatever I do, my Ultimate Purpose is to make knowledge and understanding itself a healing act. Writing this debut book in a form of a teaching memoir is my most significant action towards living out this purpose, allowing me to reach a far bigger audience than standing in front of a classroom ever could. The lessons herein will endure through time.

By this point and once done with all the steps provided above, you too should be able to summarise and articulate your purpose and life value proposition in this manner. I have included tables in the resource page to help guide you.

The Core Lessons: What to Take Away

"Embrace your rock bottom; it is the solid base upon which your new direction towards purpose is found."

The Catalyst (Chapter 5) was not a failure of my business acumen, but a **success of my soul's defence mechanism.** The pain points—anxiety, betrayal, frustration—were the precise compass readings telling me that the environment was no longer sustainable for my growth.

To ensure you successfully navigate the path from discovery to destiny, here are the three essential lessons from this journey that you must carry forward:

1. Embrace the Power of the Catalyst

The most painful moments—the burnout, the betrayal, the deep apathy—were not setbacks, but **precision-guided course corrections.** You must view your trauma and failure not as weakness, but as the *force required* to move you out of misalignment.

2. Your Purpose is a Convergence

Your calling is rarely just one thing. It's the **convergence of your unique, seemingly disparate skills** (Chapter 6). Your true purpose lies where your innate skills meet your passion and your abilities. Stop looking for a simple job title; look for a **unique, high-impact combination.**

3. Emancipate Your Identity

You must gain the courage to dismantle the outdated identity you are protecting. The title, the salary, the comfort zone—these are the shells you must shed. For me **autonomy** and **solitude** (Chapter 7) were non-negotiable needs that the corporate world could never provide. Your job now is to define your life by the **contribution you make**, not by the **credentials you hold.**

4. Don't succumb to Resistance (Chapter 8). It is proof that you are close to your calling. Find ways to help you navigate around this. You'll be happy you persisted.

Resources

Actions to Bring Your Purpose to Life

The time for reflection is over; the time for action is now. Use these steps hereunder, taken directly from my own journey, as your launch sequence:

Action Item	Description	Connection to My Story
Make Time for Introspection	Establish non-negotiable time for solitude (walking, journaling, breathwork) to quiet external noise and listen to your inner compass.	Essential to healing the burnout and discovering the **Life Path 7** traits.
Use Work and Play as	Actively test new concepts, side	**Chapter 4 (Serendipity):**

Exploratory Grounds	projects, or skills without the pressure of needing income immediately.	The Radio Frequency application and the voluntary teaching at the Church University.
Listen to Compliments (The Green Flags)	Note what people constantly ask for your help with or compliment you on, regardless of pay.	**Chapter 8:** Recognizing the inherent talent for MCing, speaking, and teaching that was previously dismissed.
Pay Attention to Your Flow State	Take note of tasks where you lose yourself entirely and time vanishes.	**Chapter 6:** The hours spent studying Phytotherapy and experimenting with herbal

		remedies felt like therapy.
Define Your Non-Negotiables	Clearly articulate the working conditions (e.g., no staff, no 9-to-5) that you need to be happy and fulfilled.	**Chapter 5:** The core need for **Autonomy** was revealed by the betrayal and the subsequent panic attacks.
Commit and Fight Resistance	Find ways to overcome psychological barriers.	**Chapter 8** teaches that you can use that as fuel to propel you forward.

Calculate your Core blueprint

Steps provided on page 148

Make a list of your talents, the skills you have acquired, and core blueprint results to see if you can map out your purpose.

Talents: Tools to fulfil your purpose	Skills: Enhance your talents	Purpose/Core blueprint: gives direction to your talents
-Natural ability -Aptitude	-Taught -Acquired through deliberate effort -Training and practise	-It is Innate -Your primary assignment -It is meant for others' benefit

Formulate Your Purpose statement

Once you have gathered all information about yourself, try to articulate your sense of purpose in a clear, concise statement. This statement should reflect your values, passions, and the legacy you want to leave behind. Keep it simple; it should resonate with you and serve as a guide in decision-making. Revisit this statement regularly to see if it still aligns with your evolving self. As you grow and experience new things, how you live out your purpose may

146

adapt as well. Embrace this evolution and remember that your purpose is a living part of who you are.

Finally, take action by setting specific goals that align with your defined purpose. Break these goals into actionable steps that can guide you in daily life. Whether it's pursuing further education, volunteering, or simply dedicating time to hobbies that bring joy. Embrace the small changes that contribute to your overall purpose. Making intentional moves towards your goals reinforces the meaning you derive from life and enhances your connection to your personal purpose. Remember, taking time to define and act on your purpose is not a luxury nor a one-time activity; it is a continuous journey that brings fulfilment and satisfaction.

All the best.

CORE BLUEPRINT CALCULATION EXAMPLE:

Life Path: Birthdate: 7 August 1977.

Step 1: Add all the numbers together

7+8+1+9+7+7= 39

3+9=12

Step 2: Reduce it further to a single digit: $1 + 2 = 3$. Refer to the Life path numbers table in chapter 7 for meaning.

Destiny/Expression: (Full Name) Tumelo Faith Moeti

Use the Number Chart (Pythagorean System) where numbers are assigned to each letter similar to a phone dial system.

1: A, J, S

2: B, K, T

3: C, L, U

4: D, M, V

5: E, N, W

6: F, O, X

7: G, P, Y

8: H, Q, Z

9: I, R

Step 1: Calculate the sum of each name

- **Tumelo**: 2 + 3 + 4 + 5 + 3 + 6 = 23.

- **Faith**: 6 + 1 + 9 + 2 + 8 = 26.

- **Moeti**: 4 + 6 + 5 + 2 + 9 = 26.

Step 2: Reduce each name sum to a single digit

- **Tumelo**: 2 + 3 = 5.

- **Faith**: 2 + 6 = 8.

- **Moeti**: 2 + 6 = 8.

Step 3: Sum the reduced numbers from each name

- 5 + 8 + 8 = 21.

Step 4: Reduce the final sum to a single digit

- 2 + 1 = **3**.

The final result, **3**, is the destiny number for Tumelo Faith Moeti.

Soul Urge: (Vowels in your name)

In Numerology, each vowel is assigned a specific numerical value as provided below:

- **A** = 1

- **E** = 5

- **I** = 9

- **O** = 6

- **U** = 3

1. Tumelo

- Vowels: U (3) + E (5) + O (6) = 14

- Reduce: 1 + 4 = **5**

2. Faith

- Vowels: A (1) + I (9) = 10

- Reduce: 1 + 0 = **1**

3. Moeti

- Vowels: O (6) + E (5) + I (9) = 20

- Reduce: $2 + 0 = 2$

4. Total Soul Urge Number

- Add the reduced numbers from each name: $5 + 1 + 2 = 8$

Numerological Aspect	Number	Core Meaning
Life Path (from birth date)	3	Tumelo's path in life: focus on creativity, self-expression, and communication.
Soul Urge (from vowels)	8	Her inner desires and motivations; focus on success, leadership, and abundance.
Destiny Expression (from full name)	3	Her natural talents and potential focus on optimism, inspiration, and social connection.

Easier method

Total Vowels: U (3) +E (5) + O (6) + A (1) + I (9) + O (6) + E (5) + I (9) = 44

- **44** is not a standard master number (11, 22, 33). reduce it further: $4 + 4 = 8$.

A summary of Tumelo Faith Moeti (born 7 August 1977):

These numbers collectively paint a picture of an ambitious individual (Soul Urge 8) who is likely to achieve their goals by utilizing strong communication skills, optimism, and creativity (Life Path 3 and Destiny Expression 3).

Thank you, dear reader.

Thank you for getting to the end of the book, my teaching memoirs. I hope you enjoyed it and found it helpful.

It had been 3 years since the ordeal that I had the urge to write this book. As captured earlier herein, healing can be long and messy. It's like a purge, a spring cleaning of the soul, but finding your Purpose doesn't always have to be like that.

If you're an professional, once you've used my guideline and discovered your Purpose

- **Refine your expertise**: Continuously hone your skills and specialization to match your purpose.
- **Strategic networking**: Cultivate and leverage professional connections.
- **Market positioning**: Effectively communicate your value proposition and expertise.
- **Establish authority**: Position yourself as a thought leader in your field.

The distinct advantage in a "soul-aligned" profession is the qualitative shift in the work experience itself—labour transforms into a pursuit of passion.

Alternatively, this alignment is attainable within an existing corporate structure. The workplace does not have to be a source of disengagement. I encourage you to proactively explore internal growth opportunities:

- **Seek internal mobility**: Petition for a transfer to a department that aligns more closely with your purpose.
- **Volunteer strategically**: Participate in cross-functional projects to gain exposure and identify a suitable organizational fit.

It's never too late to rewrite your story.

If these lessons and the GUIDED Framework herein helped you see a path toward your own purpose and a SOUL ALIGNED profession, I have one small favour to ask:

Could you take 60 seconds to leave a review on Amazon?

As an author, reviews are my lifeblood. They do two incredibly important things:

1. **They help other "burned-out" professionals** find this book and realize they aren't alone.

2. **They tell the Amazon algorithm** that this message matters, helping us reach the Best Seller charts together.

Whether it's one sentence or three paragraphs, your honest feedback makes a massive difference.

Scan QR Code, it links directly to your Amazon Review Page]

P.S. If you want to dive deeper into your Core Blueprint, don't forget to download your free **Purpose Audit Checklist** at [www.refilwemarumo.co.za/Checklist].

To your alignment and success

References

Simply Psychology. (n.d.). Erik Erikson's Stages of Psychosocial Development. Retrieved from https://www.simplypsychology.org/erik-erikson.html

South African History Online. (2016, May 6; updated 2025, November 22). A history of Apartheid in South Africa. Retrieved from https://www.sahistory.org.za/article/history-apartheid-south-africa

Stellenbosch Business School. (2024, July 1). The real costs of burnout in the workplace. Retrieved from https://www.stellenboschbusiness.ac.za/news/2024-07-01-real-costs-burnout-workplace

Psychology Today. (n.d.). Synchronicity. Retrieved from https://www.psychologytoday.com/za/basics/synchronicity

MuchSkills. (n.d.). Flexibility, diversity and continuous feedback: How millennials are changing the workplace. Retrieved from https://www.muchskills.com/blog/how-millennials-are-changing-the-workplace

QES Academy. (n.d.). How Gen Z and Millennials Are Changing the Way We Work. Retrieved from https://qesacademy.com/how-gen-z-and-millennials-are-changing-the-way-we-work/

Deloitte Insights. (2025). Gen Z and Millennial Survey. Retrieved from https://www2.deloitte.com/us/en/insights/topics/talent/2025-gen-z-millennial-survey.html

Deloitte Insights. (n.d.). It's not a stretch: Gen Z and millennials want flexibility and balance. Retrieved from https://action.deloitte.com/insight/3375/it's-not-a-stretch-gen-z-and-millennials-want-flexibility-and-balance

World Health Organization. (n.d.). Phytotherapy: The use of plants and plant extracts to treat or prevent health conditions. Retrieved from https://www.who.int

ResearchGate. (n.d.). T-shaped professional concept. Retrieved from https://www.researchgate.net

Ikigai: The Japanese secret to a long and happy life. APA. Mitsuhashi Y. (2018) Kyle books

Index